Ortus Christi

Ortus Christi

MEDITATIONS FOR ADVENT

by Mother St. Paul

Laudamus Press

Cover image: *St. John the Baptist* by Diego Polo
Cover design by Mary Jo Loboda

Interior illustrations reprinted from the Campion Missal and
Hymnal (used by permission www.ccwatershed.com), except
Madonna by Pietro Perugino and *O Antiphons.*

Laudamus Press
P.O. Box 251
Hamlin, PA 18427
www.laudamus-te.com

Preface

"Ambulabunt gentes in lumine tuo et reges in splendore ortus tui."
(Is. 9: 3).

Reading these Meditations we discover with surprise how much spiritual food is obtainable from a study of the lessons and liturgy of Advent. Mother St. Paul is always a heart-searcher. She presses self-reform upon souls, who to the eye of outward observers and perhaps in their own conceit, have little or nothing to amend. We must always be following Christ, and Christ is ever moving forward. Deliberately to stand still is to widen the distance between ourselves and Him, an ungenerous, not to say a dangerous thing to do. What are called here Meditations may well be taken for daily spiritual reading in preparation for Christmas.

Advent after all is a season of joy, and these Meditations must be taken in a joyful spirit. Courage and enthusiasm in the cause of Christ is the supreme need of all Catholics who really *love His coming.* (2 Timothy 4: 8)

JOSEPH RICKABY, S. J.
St. Beuno's College.

Note

Although there are twenty-eight Meditations given in this book they will not all be needed every year, for the length of Advent varies between twenty-two and twenty-eight days. The Third Sunday of Advent may fall as late as December 17th (the first day of the "Great O's") and the Fourth Sunday of Advent be Christmas Eve. The plan suggested, which will suit all years, is to use No. 1 on Advent Sunday and the rest according to choice till December 17th; from then to December 24th Nos. 21-28 should be used.

Contents

𝕻𝖗𝖆𝖞𝖊𝖗𝖘

Collect for the Annunciation, said at Mass every day during Advent:

> Deus, qui de beatae Mariae Virginis utero, Verbum Tuum, Angelo nuntiante, carnem suscipere voluisti: praesta supplicibus Tuis ut qui vere eam Genitricem Dei credimus, ejus apud Te intercessionibus adjuvemur.

> O God Who didst please that Thy Word should take flesh, at the message of an Angel, in the womb of the Blessed Virgin Mary; grant to Thy suppliants that we who believe her to be truly the Mother of God, may be helped by her intercession.

Collect said at Office after the *Salve Regina*:

> Omnipotens sempiterne Deus, qui gloriosae Virginis Matris Mariae corpus et animam, ut dignum Filii tui habitaculum effici mereretur, Spiritu sancto cooperante, praeparasti: da, ut cujus commemoratione laetamur, ejus pia intercessione, ab instantibus malis, et a morte perpetua liberemur.

> Almighty, everlasting God, Who by the co-operation of the Holy Ghost didst prepare the body and soul of the glorious Virgin Mother Mary to become a habitation meet for Thy Son; grant that as we rejoice in her commemoration, we may, by her loving intercession, be delivered from present evils and from everlasting death.

Little Office B. V. M. Vespers for Advent:

> Conscientias nostras, quaesumus Domine, visitando purifica, ut veniens Jesus Christus Filius Tuus Dominus noster cum omnibus Sanctis, paratam Sibi in nobis inveniat mansionem.

> Purify our consciences, we beseech Thee O Lord, by Thy visitation, that when Thy Son Jesus Christ our Lord shall come with all His Saints, He may find a mansion prepared in us for Himself.

Prayer of Venerable Father Olier

O Jesus, vivens in Maria,
Veni et vive in famulis Tuis,
In spiritu sanctitatis Tuae,
In plenitudine virtutis Tuae,
In veritate virtutum Tuarum,
In perfectione viarum Tuarum,
In communione mysteriorum Tuorum;
Dominare omni adversae potestati,
In Spiritu Tuo, ad gloriam Patris.
Amen.

O Jesus, living in Mary,
Come and live in Thy servants,
In the spirit of Thy sanctity,
In the fulness of Thy strength,
In the reality of Thy virtues,
In the perfection of Thy ways,
In the communion of Thy mysteries.
Dominate over every opposing power,
In Thine own Spirit, to the glory of the Father.
Amen.

(Indulgence: 300 days, once a day, Pius IX, Oct. 14 1859.)

From the Litany of Loreto:

Sancta Dei Genitrix, ora pro nobis. Holy Mother of God, pray for us.
Mater Christi, ora pro nobis. Mother of Christ, pray for us.
Vas spirituale, ora pro nobis. Spiritual vessel, pray for us.
Vas honorabile, ora pro nobis. Vessel of honor, pray for us.
Vas insigne devotionis, ora pro nobis. Singular vessel of devotion, pray for us.
Turris Davidica, ora pro nobis. Tower of David, pray for us.
Turris eburnea, ora pro nobis. Tower of Ivory, pray for us
Domus aurea, ora pro nobis. House of Gold, pray for us.
Foederis arca, ora pro nobis. Ark of the covenent, pray for us.
Janua coeli, ora pro nobis. Gate of heaven, pray for us

SUMENS ILLUD AVE GABRIELIS ORE, FUNDA NOS IN PACE, MUTANS EVÆ NOMEN.

RECEIVING THAT «AVE» FROM THE MOUTH OF GABRIEL, ESTAB-LISH US IN PEACE, REVERSING THE NAME OF EVE («EVA»).

Courtesy of *Campion Missal and Hymnal*

Ortus Christi

Ortus Christi

"*Arise, be enlightened, ... for thy light is come, and the glory of the Lord is **risen** upon thee.... The Lord shall **arise** upon thee ... the Gentiles shall walk in thy light, and kings in the brightness of thy rising*" (*ortus*). (Is. 40: 1-3).

1st Prelude. A picture of the first streaks of dawn.
2nd Prelude. Grace to arise because the Light has come.

POINT I.
THE RISING OF CHRIST.

The Church begins her new liturgical year with the words: "*Ad Te levavi animam meam*"—To Thee have I lifted up my soul ("Introit" for today)—as though she were straining her eyes to try to see something on the horizon. She cannot see anything very definite yet, but she is full of hope. *Deus meus, in Te confido, non erubescam*—My God I trust in Thee, let me not be ashamed, do not let me lift up my eyes in vain, she cries; and she keeps on looking. This will be her attitude all through the season of Advent, an attitude of expectancy, of waiting, of hope, of trust, of prayer. We know for what she is waiting—the *Ortus Christi*—the Rising of Christ. "The Lord shall arise upon thee" is the promise. "To Thee have I lifted up my soul" is her response. What is in her mind when she sees those first streaks of light? They are to her an earnest of what is coming, an earnest of the Advent of her Lord. St. Bernard says that His Advent is threefold, that He comes in

5

three different ways: (1) In the flesh and in weakness, (2) in the spirit and in power, (3) in glory and in majesty.

The Church knows how much these three Comings mean to her children, and so at the first sign of dawn she forgets the long weary night, and calls to each one: "*Arise*, be enlightened for thy light is come, and the glory of the Lord is risen upon thee." "Behold the Bridegroom cometh, go ye forth to meet Him."

Let us then begin our Advent in the spirit of the Church. Let us arise once more as she bids us, rouse ourselves that is, to look with her at the dawn, while we say to ourselves: "Behold He cometh leaping upon the mountains, skipping over the hills. Behold He standeth behind our wall, looking through the windows, looking through the lattices." As we look we hear the voice of our Beloved, He is speaking to His Church. What has He to say as soon as He comes in sight? "*Arise*, make haste, my love, my dove, my beautiful one, and come" (Cant. 2: 8-10). It is the same injunction: "*Arise*."

POINT II.

THE RISING OF THE CHURCH.

If the Bridegroom is rising, it is evident that the Bride must do the same. He is rising to come to His Bride, she must rise to go to Him. How? By meditating on His Advents; by thanking Him once more for them; by asking herself what use she has made of them hitherto, what use she intends to make during this New Year that is beginning; by preparing herself for them; by remembering that as His Bride she has a very real share in each.

1. The *past* Coming, "in the flesh and in weakness." We shall think about this coming more especially at Christmas, for which the season of Advent is a

preparation. "The bright and morning star" (Apoc. 22: 16) will by then have risen in all its fulness. The Word will be made Flesh and once more we shall *rise* in the "quiet silence" of the night to worship our God "in the flesh and in weakness."

2. The *present* Coming, "in the spirit and in power"—His Coming in grace to the soul, to dwell with it by His Spirit. "In *power*"—because only He Who is omnipotent could work such a stupendous miracle as the miracle of grace. This miracle could never have been worked, had it not been for the first Coming. "The Word was made Flesh" that He might by His death redeem His people and restore to them the kingdom of grace which they had lost in Adam. This second Coming is to prepare us for the third.

3. The *future* Coming, in "glory and in majesty" when He shall "come again with glory to judge both the living and the dead," and when all will be forced to *rise* and go to meet Him whether they will or not. It is those, who have *risen* voluntarily to meet their God in His second Coming, who will have no fear of the third. The second Coming, then, the Coming in grace, is the most practical one for us as we begin our Advent, and upon it we will meditate in our third Point.

POINT III.

THE DWELLING OF THE BLESSED TRINITY WITHIN US.

This is what God's Coming in grace means—a soul in the state of grace is the host of the Blessed Trinity, neither more nor less. "*We* will come to Him and will make our abode with him," (John 14: 23) and from the moment that grace enters, the soul becomes the abode of God the Father, God the Son and God the Holy Ghost.

It was at the moment of Baptism that our souls were raised to the dignity of being hosts of God Himself. What happened then? God added to the natural gifts with which He had endowed man *super*natural ones, summed up in the gift of grace. What is that? A participation in His own life, something which makes us "partakers of the *Divine* nature." (2 Pet. 1: 4). He created man thus in the beginning, for He meant man always to possess supernatural as well as natural gifts. He meant always to live with man and talk and walk with him in the paradise of his soul; but Adam chased out the Divine Guest and lost this miraculous privilege for all his children. God, however, could not rest content to be outside the souls which He had created solely that He might live in them, and He devised a way (the first Coming of Christ) by which He might get back to the dwelling which He cherished so much. We need not follow the beautiful story of the Redemption through all its wondrous steps, we know it well enough; we will take it up at Baptism, when the divine gift of life which Adam lost was restored to the soul, when God came back to His chosen dwelling, and the soul regained its responsible position of host to the Blessed Trinity. When Satan had noticed that the soul was left exposed, that it was a human soul only, with nothing divine about it, he naturally had taken possession, as he does of all empty houses; (Matt. 12: 44) so at Baptism the Priest said: "Depart from him, thou unclean spirit, and give place to the Holy Ghost." Where the Holy Ghost is, there are also the Father and the Son. The Blessed Trinity, then, waits to take possession of each soul, waits to come back to Its own, waits to restore the privilege that man had at the beginning.

Thus the new creation takes place, and the soul is no longer a human soul only, but divine, for the Divine Life within has made it one with Itself. Does man realize this privilege and rise to it? No! For the greater part of Christians we are obliged to say: No. As soon as they come to years of discretion, they invite back the unclean spirit and chase out their Divine Guest. What base ingratitude! And what folly! But God, who is rich in mercy is not repelled by such conduct; His one thought is to go back to His Temple which has been so profaned, and the scheme of Redemption included a method, (the Sacrament of Penance,) whereby, if man would, he could drive out the devil and invite back the Divine Guest. Is God angry? Does He upbraid? Does He allude to the past and throw doubts on the future? No, He *loves*, and all He asks in return is love. Such is our Guest!

Now what is my side of this great question? I am, or if I am not, I can be, a Temple of God. God is living within me. How much do I think about it? I often talk about recalling the Presence of God, but it is His Presence *within* me that I have to recall. I make Acts of Contrition, of Love. To Whom? To the God within me. Do not let me forget that my heart is an altar where I can, whenever I will, adore God. He is there to walk with me and talk to me as He did to Adam of old. He wants me to live side by side with Him, and talk to Him as naturally as I do to my friend.

Let me try this Advent, as one of the best ways of preparing for the Coming of Christ at Christmas, and for His Coming in judgment, to *realize* what the supernatural life means, what *God in me* means, what it means to be the host always of God Himself. The realization will transform my life, will alter my Point of view, will change me from a mediocre Christian into one who is filled with a great idea and who is occupied with it every moment of his time—an idea which is ever stimulating him to aim higher. *God in me*—then I am never alone, my life is intimately bound up with God's life. I am a partaker of His nature. O my God, forgive me for having thought of it so little; help me to *rise* to my great privileges. I thank Thee for letting a few streaks of Thy Divine Light reach my dark soul, and by the time that the Sun of Justice has risen in all His splendour this Advent, may my soul be flooded with the new light which the realization of the Divine Presence within it, will surely bring.

> *Colloquy.* with God within me.
>
> *Resolution.* To realize this truth today, and every day more and more.
>
> *Spiritual Bouquet.* "We will come to Him and make our abode with Him."

— ❧ —

Our Lady's Rest.

"In omnibus requiem quaesivi, et in hereditate Domini morabor."

In all these I sought rest, and I shall abide in the inheritance of the Lord. (Ecclus. 24: 11).

> *1st. Prelude.* A statue of Our Lady. (See image on the next page.)
> *2nd. Prelude.* Grace to "abide in the inheritance of the Lord."

That the Church intends us to spend the season of Advent with our Blessed Mother is quite evident to anyone who takes the trouble to study the Liturgy. The Bridegroom is coming, but it is through the Virgin-Mother that He will come; and if we would be amongst the first to greet Him, if we desire a large share of His grace, if we would have no fear of His judgments, we must keep close to Mary.

POINT I.
"I SHALL ABIDE IN THE INHERITANCE OF THE LORD."

The Church applies these words to Mary; let us try to see what they mean and how far we may copy her in her determination. "The inheritance of the Lord," what is it? The words bear many interpretations but we cannot be wrong, surely, in thinking that this inheritance was Mary's own soul; it was indeed "the inheritance of the Lord," an inheritance to which the Blessed Trinity had a special right, the Father because He had created her in grace, the Son because He had saved her from the stain of original sin, the Holy Ghost because He had ever sanctified her and kept her "full of grace." But what was it that made *this* inheritance more pleasing to God than any of the other souls which He had redeemed? Mary's correspondence with grace we naturally answer; but what do we mean by that? We mean, or we ought to mean, that Mary realized to the full that God the Father, God the Son and God the Holy Ghost lived within her; and hence her resolution to abide in "the inheritance of the Lord," never to leave her Divine Guest, never to forget that she was the host and that it was her privilege to entertain. This is surely the secret of Mary's life and of her correspondence with grace. She dwelt in closest union with the God who dwelt within her.

POINT II.
"IN ALL THINGS I SOUGHT REST."

Where did she seek this rest, this calm of which her whole life speaks? Within her own soul with her Divine Guest, in other words Mary lived an *interior* life. She preferred a life inside with God, to one outside in the world. Hers was a continual realization of God's Presence—of God's Presence within her; and it was this realization which enabled her to find rest in every circumstance of her chequered life. She did not allow outward events to mar her interior calm. Her Divine Guest was always there and to Him she could always turn. The consequence was that she was never agitated, disquieted, excited, anxious, troubled. She dwelt "in the inheritance of the Lord," and there she sought rest in all things whether it was in:

- The joy of the Archangel's visit, or the difficulty of her visit to Elizabeth.
- The anguish of the reception at Bethlehem, or the joy at the birth of her Son.
- The Angels who sang: *Glorias* at His birth, or the neighbours who made unkind remarks.
- The shepherds who came to worship in their poverty, or the Wise Men in all their pomp and splendour.
- The ecstasy caused by her Babe's smile, or the distress caused by His tears.
- The words of the Angel: "Of His Kingdom there shall be no end," or the words of Simeon: He shall be "a sign which shall be contradicted."
- The peaceful home-life with JESUS and Joseph, or the hurried flight into Egypt.
- The anguish of losing Him (Desolation), or the joy of finding Him (Consolation).
- The active work for the little household, or the times of contemplation at JESUS' feet.
- The long, happy days at Nazareth with her Son, or the sad day when He left His Mother's roof.
- The account of His success: "All men go to Him," or the account of His failure: "They all forsook Him and fled."
- The cry: "Hosannah, blessed is He!" or the cry: "Crucify Him, crucify Him! it is not fit that He should live."

- The agony of watching Him suffer and die, or the delight of seeing His glorified Body.
- The pain of being left in exile on earth, or the joy of hearing Him say: "Arise, My fair one and come, the winter is over."

*　*　*　*　*

In omnibus requiem quaesivi.—Not that all these things were the same to her, not that she was indifferent or did not care, she cared more than anyone else could, for her heart was perfect and therefore more delicate and sensitive than any other except the Sacred Heart of JESUS. What then was her secret? That she lived with the Blessed Trinity, and that made her see God's Will in all that happened to her, and see it so vividly that she almost lost sight of the particular circumstances, and hardly knew whether they were painful or joyful. The pain was a joy because it was God's Will, and the joy was only a joy because it was God's Will; so she never wanted to change any thing. She sought rest in the holy habitation, the home of the Blessed Trinity; she pondered things over in her heart, that is, she talked about them with her Divine Guest.

POINT III.

THE CHILD OF MARY.

The child must copy the Mother. How is it with me? Surely if anyone ought to realize the Divine Presence within, it is a child of Mary! How far do I copy Our Lady in her interior life? What do I know of that deep calm within, into which I can always retire and seek rest, and where I can, if I will, rest so entirely that outward circumstances make little difference? If I have made the same resolution as Our Lady; namely, to "abide in the inheritance of the Lord;" pain and anxiety and difficulty will be an actual source of joy, because they afford an excuse for an extra visit to the Home within, and for longer conversations than usual with my loved Guest. If a difficulty or a humiliation or something that I do not like comes in my way, I shall not be troubled, my first thought will be with my Divine Guest. *He* has permitted this, even planned it. I will go and talk to Him about it, find out what He means, what He wants me to do and how I can best act in the circumstances to gain glory for Him. This is what is meant by the interior life, and it *can* be, it *ought* to be, far stronger than the exterior. It means a holy indifference to everything except God's Will; it means rest and peace about everything that happens, without any desire to have things altered; it takes all anxiety and disquiet and perplexity out of life and leaves a great calm which nothing has the power to disturb *except* a will in opposition to God's Will.

In omnibus requiem quaesivi.—Is it so very hard? Perhaps, for it means the spiritual life, and that means a continual battle against self; but it is a battle worth fighting. To fight is not only the way to "*seek* rest," but it is also the surest way to obtain it; for they alone who are continually fighting to keep the enemy out can hope to detain their Divine Guest within.

Colloquy with Mary. Help me, my Mother, to dwell, this Advent, in "the inheritance of the Lord," and when outward things are too much for me and I am apt to behave in a manner unworthy of a child of thine, do thou lead me by the hand into the place of rest and calm, where God Himself dwells, and where I shall see things from His Point of view.

"O God, who didst please that Thy Word should take flesh, at the message of an angel, in the womb of the Blessed Virgin Mary, grant to Thy suppliants, that we who believe her to be truly

the Mother of God may be helped by her intercession." (Collect to be said every day at Mass
from Advent to Christmas Eve.)

Resolution. To "abide in the inheritance of the Lord"
today.

Spiritual Bouquet. "In all things I sought rest."

— ❦ —

My Sins—A Triptych.

*"The night is past, and the day is at hand; let us therefore   cast
off the works of darkness and put on the armour of light."* (From the
"Epistle" for the First Sunday of Advent).

> *1st. Prelude.* The Foot of the Cross where my sins have all been laid.
> *2nd. Prelude.* The grace of contrition and firm resolution.

It is clear from the words which she has chosen for her
"Epistle" for the First Sunday of Advent that the Church
intends us during this solemn season to think about sin,—
the darkness of the past night and the light of the day that
is coming and our duty with regard to both. It is not sin in
the abstract, but our own personal sins that we are to consider. "Let *us* cast off the works of darkness." If the Apostle
Paul included himself in that "*us*," we need not fear to do
the same. It is meet, when we are thinking on the one hand
of Him Who is coming to save us from our sins and on the
other of His coming to judge us "according to our works,"
that we should give some thought to those sins. Nothing will
better help us to understand the mercy of the Saviour and
the justice of the Judge than a meditation upon our own sins.
God *forgets* the sins He has forgiven, but it is better for us,
more wholesome and more humiliating, to remember them
sometimes. David says: "My sin is always before me" (Ps. 50: 5).

The object of this meditation, then, is not to cause trouble in the soul—trouble about sins that are *forgiven* can only come from the devil—but to excite in us a deeper contrition, more gratitude and a greater watchfulness.

Point I.

A Triptych—My Sins.

Am I to consider all the sins of my life? The subject seems so vast, it is difficult to know how to condense it so that I may be able to bring it within my grasp. All sin may be summed up in one word—disobedience—*non serviam*. It was the sin of the Angels, it was the sin of our first parents and it is at the root of every sin that has ever been committed. God says: Thou shalt not, the sinner says: I will. God says: Do this and thou shalt live; the sinner says: I will not, I would rather die. Sin is man's will in opposition to God's Will. This thought simplifies the subject and makes it easier for me to call up the sins of my life and look at them. Let me make a picture of them—a triptych, a picture, that is, with three panels side by side, the middle one shall be called *Places*, that on the right hand *Persons* and that on the left *Work*.

1. *Places.* As I look at the middle picture I see it consists of numbers and numbers of small ones, each representing some place that is familiar to me—there is the house where I was born, there the school I attended, houses I have visited, hotels where I have stayed, gardens, playgrounds, lonely roads, walks on cliffs, villages, towns, churches, the sea-side, trams, omnibuses, trains, boats, bicycles, carriages, stations.... I am fascinated and cannot help looking still, though the variety and number are almost bewildering. Each picture is so familiar; some awaken sweet and

precious memories, from some I quickly turn away my eyes. All can witness to my presence, how many can witness also to my sins? "Indeed the Lord is in this place, and *I knew it not.*" (Gen. 28: 16). That may to some extent be true and if so there is One who is always ready to say: "Father, forgive them for they know not what they do." *I* know how much I knew, and the best thing, the only thing for me to do is to make an Act of Contrition.

2. *Persons.* I turn to the right hand panel and there are crowds and crowds of *faces*, each one familiar—father, mother, brothers, sisters, relations, servants, teachers, scholars, friends, enemies, priests, confessors, acquaintances ... what impression have I left upon each of these? If they could be called up and asked: "What did you think of so and so?" what would they have to say? They would have something, for I left *some* impression—and yet *none* of them know me as I really am. The three Persons of the Blessed Trinity have been near me *always* and always observant. They really know me. What have *They* to say? "If Thou, O Lord, wilt mark iniquities, Lord, who shall stand it?" (Ps. 129: 3).

    This picture makes me sad! That is just what Our Lord wants from this meditation. Let me offer once more my heartfelt contrition and He will be glad that I had the courage to open the triptych.

3. *Work.* As I turn to the panel on the left I feel that I can breathe more freely—my work will certainly give satisfaction! It is something to be proud of; I have always got on well; I have never been idle and I have had a certain measure of success, and I feel that in that respect at any rate my life will bear inspection. But

this picture too, as I look at it, seems to be divided up. Yes, I can see quite clearly all the different works upon which I have been engaged. All are very familiar and bring back for the most part happy memories, but some of them seem to be labelled.—What is it that is written across them? *"You did it to Me."* And all the rest that have no labels? They do not count—so evidently considered the One Who put on the labels. He left them, passed them over, there was nothing there *for Him.* But that hospital that was founded is not labelled, nor that legacy promised for a charitable purpose! Surely some of these without labels are "good works!" And these that are labelled are such insignificant things, things I should never have remembered at all if they were not in the picture—a kind word, a smile, a hasty word kept back because I knew it would pain *Him,* suffering cheerfully borne because I wanted to be like Him who suffered for me. Why these and not those? Because He prefers *little* things? No, but because of the motive. Had the hospital been built out of love for Him and His sick, had it been built for the glory of God and not for the glory of self, it too would have been labelled. Had the hasty word been kept back that others might notice my self-control, it would *not* have been labelled. What counts with God is the intention with which a thing is done. If it is done out of love for Him, no matter how insignificant it is, yea, no matter how badly done, it will surely be labelled *"You did it to Me,"* and it will last when the mighty works that men have so much praised are crumbling in the dust, labelled with another label *You did it not unto Me.* Have I not need to make another Act of Contrition as I think of my works, my love of gain, my ambition, love of praise and success, of the motives of my so-called works of charity, of the times in which I have allowed my work to take the first place in my life, while my soul had to take the second?

I shut up my triptych and leave it at Thy Feet O my JESUS, where the Blood from Thy Wounds may ever drip upon it, while I with Magdalen stoop and bathe Thy Feet with my tears.

POINT II.

THE TRIPTYCH.—GOD'S MERCIES.

As I look up, I see my triptych opened again and all the thousands of little pictures seem to be transformed. Each one is speaking to me of God's goodness and tenderness and love. How good it is to turn away from my own misery to His infinite mercy; yea, more—to recognize that the one is the cause of the other! And this is what He wants. If the sight of self does not lead me instinctively to look at Christ, it is a very dangerous thing, for it can only lead to despondency and discouragement. The object of looking at self and its deeds is so to look that everything good or evil may shrivel up and disappear, till self is there no longer, but Christ only and all *He* has done either for or through me. As I gaze now at the picture, I no longer see the places on earth which have known me for short periods of time, but my place in Heaven which by His mercy, if I persevere to the end, is to know me through all eternity; not my dear ones as I saw them on earth, but as they are now in my heavenly country waiting for me; not my innumerable sins of omission, nor my "good works" done to please self, but the work of Him who always pleased His Father, work which has made up for all my omissions, and which shines through every thing that I have done for Him, making it, too, acceptable to His Father. It seems to me now that I want to linger over the picture, for His mercies are indeed infinite, and I shall never be able to thank Him enough for them.

But does He, the God of infinite mercy and plenteous redemption, never look at my pictures? He says: "I will forgive their iniquity, and I will remember their sin no more" (Jer. 31: 34); and it is true. He will never open my triptych for the sake of looking at my sins, but may He not open it for the joy of seeing each of those thousands of pictures shining with pearls—the tears of contrition? Do not let me disappoint Him. This is the chalice of consolation which I can offer to the Sacred Heart in reparation.

> *Colloquy* with JESUS thanking Him for making me look at my triptych and for all that He has taught me in it.
>
> *Resolution. Never to look at my sins without at once seeing Christ*—a sight which will necessarily produce humility, gratitude and contrition.
>
> *Spiritual Bouquet.* "My sin is always before me" but "Thou shalt give joy and gladness.... and my mouth shall declare Thy praise" (Ps. 50: 5, 10, 17).

— ❧ —

The Last Judgment.

"The powers of Heaven shall be moved; and then shall they see the Son of Man coming in a cloud with great power and majesty." (The "Gospel" for the 1st. Sunday of Advent.)

1st. Prelude. The Last Day.
2nd. Prelude. Grace to meditate upon it.

The Church invites us during Advent to turn our thoughts towards the Second Coming of Christ—His Coming in judgment at the end of the world. The subject of the Last Judgment is perhaps one which we are rather inclined to avoid in our Meditations; but it is one about which Our Blessed Lord said a great deal; it is continually mentioned, too, in the Epistles and in the Apocalypse, and as we shall most certainly take a part in that last great scene of the world's drama, it is surely well for us to have a rehearsal from time to time.

POINT I.

THE COMING OF THE JUDGE.

When will He come? God "hath *appointed* a day wherein He will judge the world in equity by the Man whom He hath appointed." (Acts 18: 31). The day then is *fixed*, "but of that day and hour no one knoweth, no not the Angels of Heaven, but the Father alone." (Matt. 24: 36).

How will He come? He "shall so come as you have seen Him going into Heaven" (Acts 1: 11), the Angel told the Apostles who had just watched His Ascension. He will come, that is, in His beautiful Resurrection Body, dazzling with brightness and glory, with the wounds in Hands and Feet and Side. He will come "with much power and majesty" (Matt. 24: 30) for He will come to judge, not to preach penance nor atone for sin; He will come unexpectedly "as a thief in the night" (1 Thess. 5: 2) "at what hour you think not" (Luke 12: 40); He will come "with thousands of His Saints" (Jude 14) for all those "who have slept through JESUS will God bring with Him" (1 Thess. 4: 13); He will bring, too, "all the Angels with Him" (Matt. 25: 31); He will come "with the voice of an Archangel, and with the trumpet of God" (1 Thess. 4: 15); He will come "with the clouds" (Apoc. 1: 7); He will come "in the glory of His Father with His Angels"

(Matt. 16: 27); He will come "as lightning" (24: 27) and before Him will come His Cross—"the sign of the Son of man" in the heavens (verse 30), every eye shall see it. What different emotions that sign will excite!

POINT II.
THE EFFECTS OF HIS COMING.

"Every eye shall see Him, and they also that pierced Him. And all the tribes of the earth shall bewail themselves because of Him" (Apoc. 1: 7).

"We shall all rise again." (1 Cor. 15: 51).

"The sea will give up the dead that are in it, and death and hell ... their dead that are in them." (Apoc. 20: 13).

"The dead who are in Christ shall rise first." (1 Thess. 4: 15).

"We shall be changed, for this corruptible must put on incorruption, and this mortal must put on immortality." (1 Cor. 15: 52).

"He shall send His Angels with a trumpet, and a great voice, and they shall gather together His elect from the four winds." (Matt. 24: 31).

"Then we who are alive, who are left, shall be caught up together with them (those who died in Christ) in the clouds to meet Christ." (1 Thess. 4: 16).

"Then shall He sit upon the seat of His Majesty," (Matt. 25: 31) *and "render to every man according to his works."* (chap. 16: 27).

Then *"the heavens shall pass away with great violence, and the elements shall be melted with heat, and the earth and the works which are in it shall be burnt up."* (2 Pet. 3: 10). *And all these events are to take place "in a moment, in the twinkling of an eye!"* (1 Cor. 15: 52).

With the vivid words of Scripture before us, it is not difficult to make a picture of the scene—the sign of the Cross where all can see it; the voice of the Archangel and the trumpet of God heralding the approach of the Judge; the Son of Man, coming in the clouds with all His Angels and thousands of His Saints (all those from Heaven and Purgatory); the cries of those to whom His coming is as that of "a thief in the night" (1 Thess. 5: 2); the shouts of joy of "the children of light" (verse 5); the opening of the graves, the sea giving up its dead and the reunion of each soul, whether from Heaven, Purgatory or hell, with its body; the changing of the bodies of those who are living on the earth into Resurrection bodies; then the great multitude of the elect clothed in their bodies of immortality rising to meet their Lord in the air; then "the great white throne" set up and He who is "appointed by God to be Judge" (Acts 10: 42) taking His seat upon it, "His garment ... white as snow ... His throne like flames of fire ... thousands of thousands" ministering to Him (Dan. 7: 9, 10); the dead, great and small, standing in the presence of the throne (Apoc. 20: 12), "ten thousand times a hundred thousand" standing before Him. (Dan. 7: 10).

POINT III.

THE JUDGMENT.

(1) *The Separation.* Quickly the Angels separate that vast multitude into two companies—those on His right Hand and those on His left, the sheep and the goats, those who are to enter into life everlasting and those who are to enter into everlasting punishment (Matt. 25: 46); those who have been faithful over the few things entrusted to them and those who have hidden their Lord's talent; those whose lamps are burning and those whose lamps are going out. There is fixed a great chaos between the two companies, so that they

who would pass from one side to the other *cannot*, it is too late. (Luke 16: 26).

(2) *The books.* "And the books were opened ... and the dead were judged by those things which were written in the books, according to their works." "And another book was opened, which is the book of life," and only "they that are written in the book of life of the Lamb" shall enter Heaven. (Apoc. 20: 12, 21: 27). "Every man's work shall be manifest" (1 Cor. 3: 13); "every idle word that men shall speak, they shall render an account for it in the day of Judgment" (Matt. 12: 36). Then will be seen, and all will acknowledge it, the triumph of right over wrong, the triumph of the Kingdom, the triumph of Christ; then will be adjusted all that we have so often longed to adjust but could not, for "let both grow together till the harvest" was the King's order. Then will seeming injustices be explained and crimes that have called to Heaven for vengeance receive their just reward. Then will the unanimous cry be: "The Lord He is God," and all will be forced to add: "He doeth all things well."

(3) *The Sentences.* There are only two: (1) "Then shall the King say to them that shall be on His right Hand: Come, ye blessed of my Father, possess you the kingdom prepared for you from the foundation of the world." He tells them why they are to have such a blessed reward—they have been faithful subjects of their King during their lives on earth, they have ministered to His needs, lived for Him and not for self. They seem surprised, they cannot remember doing acts of charity to their King and He explains: "As long as you did it to one of these My least brethren, you did it to Me." (Matt. 25: 40). The sentence

"Come" is pronounced on those who lived their lives for their King, who did all they had to do, no matter what it was, for Him, thus uniting themselves with Him, and now He will unite Himself with them for all eternity—"*Come!*"

(2) "Then He shall say to them also that shall be on His left Hand: Depart from Me, you cursed, into everlasting fire." And again He gives His reasons for this terrible punishment—they would not acknowledge Him as their King, would not serve Him, lived for self instead of for Him and His brethren: "As long as you did it *not* to one of these least, neither did you do it to Me" (verse 45). During their lives they separated themselves from the King and His interests: "We will not have this Man to reign over us;" now He will separate Himself from them for all eternity.— "*Depart from Me!*"

Then He "will say to the reapers: Gather up first the cockle, and bind it into bundles to burn, but the wheat gather ye into My barn." (Matt. 13: 30). "The Angels shall go out, and shall separate the wicked from among the just, and shall cast them into the furnace of fire" (verses 49, 50). "Then shall the just shine as the sun in the Kingdom of their Father. He that hath ears to hear let him hear" (verse 43).

Colloquy. Inter oves locum praesta, Et ab hoedis me sequestra, Statuens in parte dextra. (Among the sheep grant me a place, separate me from the goats, placing me on Thy right Hand).

Resolution. To remember "the doctrine ... of eternal judgment" (Heb. 6: 2) today.

Spiritual Bouquet. "He shall come again to judge the living and the dead."

— ❧ —

Traders and Talents.

"A man going into a far country called his servants and delivered to them his goods; and to one he gave five talents, and to another two, and to another one, to every one according to his proper ability; and immediately he took his journey." (Matt. 25: 14).

1st. Prelude. JESUS telling this parable to His disciples.
2nd. Prelude. Grace to learn the lessons from it which He intended.

POINT I.
THE TALENTS.

It is Christ Himself Who is the Author of this parable and He told it to show us how we are to prepare for His Coming. Every word of it is of importance and bears some instruction or warning for Advent.

The *"man going into a far country"* is the Man-God, He Who came from Heaven to take our human nature and to redeem us to God by His Blood. His work of Redemption is finished and He is going back to His own country—*"A far country"*—implying that He will be gone a long time.

(He) *"called His servants."* They are His own servants, He has created them, He has bought them with His Blood, they belong to Him—their service, their time, their very lives are His, and this not because they are *slaves* forced to labour, but because of their own free will and out of love and gratitude to Him who has bought them from the cruel slavery of sin, they have said: "I love my Master ... I will not go out free" (Ex. 21: 5).

"And (He) delivered to them His goods." They are *His* goods not the servants', they all belong to Him and He entrusts them to His servants to take care of them and to do the best they

can with them while He is gone. What are these "goods?" All the good things which God has given to man—his life, his preservation, his Baptism, his christian education, intellect, faith, health, rank, wealth, talents, conscience, opportunities of doing good, position,—and all have to be traded with, for the Master to Whom they belong. His "goods" include too what the world would label "evils"—ill-health, difficulty, failure, poverty, incapability; these have to be traded with too, and there is often a higher profit to be made out of these than out of the others. They are all the Master's goods and He delivers them to His servants.

"To one He gave five talents and to another two and to another one, to every one according to his proper ability." He knows His servants, and He knows exactly the strength and capability of each. He measures each burden before imposing it and calculates each sum before giving it. This servant can manage five, this one two, this can only manage one. It is no disgrace to have only one talent, the ability of the servants is the Master's affair, not the servants'. They cannot turn to Him and say: "Why hast Thou made me thus?" (Rom. 9: 20). He makes each one according to His own Will and endows him according to His Will too. What the servant has to remember is that he is responsible for all that is entrusted to him, that he *can* trade with it and that it is not too much for him, it is "according to his proper ability," and that though his Master will never try to reap where He has not sown, He *will* expect to reap where He *has* sown, He will expect a harvest from each talent.

Point II.
The Traders.

"*He that had received the five talents went his way and traded with the same and gained other five.*" He lost no time, he loved his Master and he loved the "goods" because they belonged to his Master and because they had been lent by Him. The whole of their value lay in the fact that they were the Master's; he felt responsible, he must not only take care of them but put them to the best account, and so he set to work at once to trade with them, and he did well, for he gained *cent per cent*!

"*And in like manner he that had received the two gained other two.*" There was no jealousy, no thinking the Master partial or that He had underrated his powers in only giving him *two* talents. He loved and trusted his Master; the two talents were very precious because they were His and because He had chosen them out with such love and care, giving the servant just what he could manage, no more and no less. He went and traded and did as well as the first, *cent per cent*.

Thus the good servants, that is those who love, who have said, I *will* not go out free, are always trading for their Master. They say to themselves: This talent, this time, this opportunity, this health, this strength belongs to my Master not to me, I must use it for Him. They forget sometimes; the Master is so long away and they act as if the goods were their own, and even trade with them for their own profit, using their talents to attract people to themselves rather than to their Master! But as they really love Him and want to "trade" for Him only, they see the dishonesty of their trading and they do their best by acts of reparation to restore to Him His own. When He comes back, He will not expect perfection but *effort*. Some, He says, will gain "a hundred fold" but for our consolation and encouragement He adds: "some sixty-fold, and some thirtyfold" (Matt. 13: 8).

"*But he that had received the one, going his way digged into the earth, and hid his lord's money.*" He lost no time either, his mind was made up at once, he would take no trouble, make no effort, would hide his Master's talent and forget all about it; he wanted no responsibility, he could not be troubled with "trading." His Master could not expect much from him, he argued, because he had entrusted so little to him, he knew he was not capable of doing *much*, but he would do nothing at all. He did not waste or spoil his Master's goods, his sin was one of *omission*—you did it *not* to Me. He dug in the earth instead of laying up treasure in Heaven.

POINT III.

THE RECKONING.

"*After a long time the Lord of those servants came and reckoned with them.*" Each servant must come up before Him to give an account and to be judged according to his works.

"*Lord, Thou didst deliver to me five talents, behold I have gained other five over and above.*"

"*Lord, Thou deliveredst two talents to me, behold I have gained other two.*" The Lord gives exactly the same answer, the same reward to each, showing clearly that what counts in the reckoning is not the *number* of good works but the spirit and intention and motive with which they are done, be they many or few.

"*Well done, good and faithful servant, because thou hast been faithful over a few things, I will place thee over many things.*" The reward is not given to the most capable, nor to those who have the most or the greatest talents, but to those who have been *faithful* over the few things entrusted to them.

They have traded with their talents for God's glory and for the salvation of their own souls. They have realized that each thing entrusted to them was a "good," whether it was sickness or health, poverty or riches, prosperity or adversity, and they have said about each: This belongs to the Master, how can I best use it for Him? Now they find that the merit of each action done, each suffering borne for Him, has been carefully stored up.

"*Enter thou into the joy of thy Lord.*" It is His joy, His interest, His glory that the faithful servant has studied on earth, now he shall share them for ever.

"*He that had received the one talent came and said: Lord, I know that Thou art a hard man*" expecting the impossible, "*and being afraid I went and hid Thy talent in the earth; behold here Thou hast that which is Thine.*" He could have traded and made *cent per cent* as the others had done and earned the "*Euge*" ("Well done!") He not only did not do this, but he put all the blame on his Master Who with such care had given him just the talent that was suited to his ability. He was *afraid*, he said, afraid of what? Of his Master because He was hard and unjust? No, this was only an excuse, he knew his Master and he knew it was not true. What he was afraid of was hard work, effort, ceaseless watching against temptation. It was far less irksome to bury the talent and live a life of ease, letting things just take their course, and hoping all would come out right in the end; but at the end things were not right, for he had nothing to give to his Master, the one talent *was* the Master's, he knew that quite well: "Behold here Thou hast that which is Thine."

"*Wicked and slothful servant*"—wicked, because he had robbed God of His rights; slothful, because he would not raise a finger to serve his Master.

"*Take ye away therefore the talent from him and give it him that hath ten.*" It is a solemn thought that a grace refused by one may be handed on to another who is more faithful.

"*To everyone that hath shall be given*" is a principle of the Kingdom. He ever giveth "grace for grace" (John 1: 16). For every grace used He gives "more grace"—"he shall abound."

"*From him that hath not, that also which he seemeth to have shall be taken away.*" There is such a thing as a last grace, a last opportunity. God has nowhere pledged Himself to give the grace of repentance; grace is ever a free gift and He is not unjust if He withholds it. I can never say: I will sin and repent after! To sin is in my power, but to repent is not. Our Lord speaks of sinners filling up the measure of their iniquity (Matt. 23: 32). Had Herod reached the limit, filled up the measure? Is that why Our Lord refused to speak to him? We do not know, but we do know that it is possible for a sinner to sin to such an extent—not necessarily by gross sin, but by steadily refusing God's grace and the opportunities offered to him—that what he has, that is, his opportunities, will be taken from him.

"*The unprofitable servant cast ye out into the exterior darkness.*" He ever shunned the light and now it will *never* be his. He was *unprofitable*, that was his sin, he did nothing for his Master. All sins, however terrible, will be forgiven if the sinner turns to God and repents, because his repentance shows that he is "trading," though he may often fail in his business; but the unprofitable servant carries on no trade with God at all, he leaves Him out altogether. There is nothing for God to do but to leave him out in the "exterior darkness" which he has deliberately chosen.

Colloquy with the Master, Who though He is a "long time" coming, is never far from those who are trading for Him.

Resolution. Never to leave the Master out of anything I do.
Spiritual Bouquet. "Well done good and faithful servant!"

— ❧ —

Stir Up!

"I think it meet ... to stir you up by putting you in   *remembrance."* (2 Pet. 1: 13).

1st. Prelude. Paul writing to Timothy: "Stir up the grace of God which is in thee" (2 Tim. 1: 6).
2nd. Prelude. Grace to stir myself up this Advent.

On the Sunday before Advent and nine times during the Advent Masses, the Church puts on the lips of her children this prayer: *Stir up, O Lord.* Let us try in this Meditation to catch her spirit which runs all through the Advent season and see what it is that she wants God to stir up.

POINT I.
HIS OWN MIGHT.

We ask Him during Advent to stir up His might for four different reasons.
(1) *To protect and deliver us.* "Stir up Thy might, we beseech Thee O Lord and come: that by Thy protection we may deserve to be delivered from the threatening dangers of our sins and by Thy deliverance be saved." (The "Collect" for Advent Sunday.)
We ask Him to show His might by *protecting* us from dangers and by *delivering* us from sin. We want to spend a good Advent, we want to prepare well for His Coming, then there rise up before us the "threatening dangers of our sins"—those old temptations that

33

are sure to come back again as soon as we begin to put forth fresh effort. Are we to be discouraged, to dread them, to say we are sure to fall again, and thus give the enemy a hold over us? No, but to believe that our God Who is coming will protect us in the day of battle, that though to humiliate and to strengthen us, He may still permit the temptations, yet He will Himself be our shield and buckler, and will deliver us if we trust in His strength and not in our own—"Stir up Thy might, O Lord, and come to protect and deliver."

(2) *To free us from adversity.* "Stir up Thy power, we beseech Thee O Lord and come, that they who confide in Thy mercy may be more speedily freed from all adversity" (The "Collect" for Friday in Ember week). The adversity from which the Church prays to be freed here is probably the same as she continually teaches us to pray for deliverance from in her Litanies: war, pestilence, famine, floods, earthquakes— all things which damage the peace of nations and the produce of the earth, great national disasters. From all such the world will never be free till the Advent of her Lord, till God stirs up His power and comes to save it. Meanwhile for our consolation we can remember that it is when God's judgments are in the earth that the nations learn justice (Isaias 26: 9). Adversity is a great teacher and trainer for Heaven, and as we advance in the spiritual life we see more and more that many things which are adversity to the body are prosperity to the soul. We should naturally like to be freed from the adversity of sickness, poverty, failure, loss of friends, of health and strength, but all these adversities have their work to do. "These are they who came out of great tribulation," and it is probable

that but for the tribulation many would never "have washed their robes and have made them white in the blood of the Lamb" (Apoc. 7: 14). Let us strive to be amongst those who *trust* Him, who *confide* in His mercy, who believe that He knows what is best for them, and who gladly let Him arrange all for them. He *will* stir up His power and speedily free them one day, but it will not be till the flail of adversity has done its work and the corn is ready to be garnered in the heavenly barns.

(3) *To save us.* "Stir up Thy might O Lord and come to save us."

In the Masses for the third week, that is Ember week, the prayer occurs five times, twice in the Mass for the third Sunday and three times in that for Ember Saturday. The time of the birth of the Saviour is drawing nearer, and the Church is beginning to be importunate. Stir up Thy *might*; for though He is coming as a little helpless infant, He is God "mighty to save."

(4) *To accelerate His Coming.* "Stir up Thy might, we beseech Thee O Lord and come; and succour us with great power, that by the help of Thy grace, the indulgence of Thy mercy may accelerate what our sins impede." (The "Collect" for the 4th. Sunday of Advent).

We ask Him to stir up His might in *coming*. His Advents show His Omnipotence. Only a *God* could come to this world to save it, only a *God* could come to a soul and raise it to the supernatural state. These are miracles and we ask Him to stir up His might to come and work them. It is our sins that hold Him back and hinder His work both in our own souls and in the world. We want them to do so no more and so we ask for His succour and indulgence.

POINT II.
OUR WILLS.

"Stir up the wills of Thy faithful, O Lord, we beseech Thee; that earnestly seeking after the fruit of good works, they may receive more abundant helps from Thy mercy." (The "Collect" for the Sunday before Advent).

Here we pray for something which it is far more difficult to "stir up"—our own wills. We are not sufficiently in earnest; the might and the mercy of God are there waiting to help us, but we have not the energy nor the desire to receive them. We weaken our wills by yielding to temptation, by deliberately going into occasions of sin, by allowing ourselves to be careless about rules and resolutions, by letting things drift and contenting ourselves with a low standard. Advent is a time to rectify all this, to pull ourselves up and make a fresh start, and if we are in earnest, we shall gladly join in the prayer: "Stir up the wills of Thy faithful, O Lord," stir up *my* will. It is not a prayer to be said lightly for it means much—a will stirred up to "seek after the fruit of good works" means constant and continued effort; it means mortification, suffering, death to self; it means a determination to do or suffer *anything* rather than run the *least* risk of committing the *least* sin; it means constant unremitting attention to little things— to the smallest duties, the least prickings of conscience; it means hard work. *Dare* I say this prayer? If I am *really* anxious for "the fruit of good works," I shall dare anything. Fruit is impossible without hard work either in the natural or the spiritual world.

"Who is sufficient for these things?" Certainly I am not, but the consolation is that the work is *co-operative*. As soon as I pray: Stir up my will, O God, because I want to bring forth fruit to Thy glory; He will be there giving me *"more abundant helps"* from His mercy. God does not expect me to work alone, nor to suffer alone, nor to make efforts alone. What He wants is a good will. He is coming "to men of good will," and nothing can prove that I am one of them, better than a fervent prayer that my will may be stirred up, cost what it may. The "abundant helps" will immediately be at my service; and when it seems sometimes as if, in spite of all my efforts, the day is going to be lost, I will hold on still, remembering that the help is *"more* abundant" when the need is greater. The stores of His mercy are infinite and He ever gives *more* to the generous soul.

POINT III.

OUR HEARTS.

"Stir up our hearts, O Lord, to prepare the ways of Thy only-begotten Son: that by His Coming we may be worthy to serve Thee with purified minds." (The "Collect" for the 2nd Sunday of Advent).

Here lies the secret; if our *hearts* are stirred up there will be little difficulty about our *wills*. If I *love*, I shall gladly make efforts, no trouble will be too much, no work too exacting, no sacrifice too great, no mortification too hard. *"If you love Me, keep My commandments."* My will is to be stirred up to *seek*, but my heart is to be stirred up to *prepare*. It is my King Who is coming, He Who has a right to my heart, and He is quite sure to pass by my way, for to win my heart and make it all His own is one of the special reasons of His Coming. No pains, no cost shall be spared in my preparation; my heart shall be decorated with the flowers that I know He loves and hung with banners which shall speak of my gratitude for all He has done. This is the preparation of the heart—the preparation of *love*; and it will not stop at my own heart, for if I really love my King I shall take an interest in all the work that

He is coming to do; I shall try to prepare His way for Him in the hearts of others; I shall let them know that JESUS of Nazareth is going to pass by. Perhaps I shall have no opportunity of speaking about His visit, but the careful preparations I am making will not go unnoticed—each thing that I do out of love to Him will in some way or another spread His Kingdom in the hearts of men.

Colloquy. With my King Who is coming.

Resolution. To do something *today* in preparation.

Spiritual Bouquet. "Stir up!"

— ❦ —

St. John The Baptist. (1)
His Preparation.

"This is he of whom it is written: Behold I send my Angel before Thy face, who shall prepare Thy way before Thee." (Matt. 11: 10).

1st. *Prelude.* Picture of the Naming Day of St. John the Baptist who is on Our Lady's knee, while Elizabeth and the kinsfolk are discussing the name and Zachary is writing on a tablet; St. Joseph is looking on.

2nd. *Prelude.* The spirit of penance.

Often during Advent the Church directs our thoughts to the great Precursor of JESUS Christ, to him who was sent to prepare His ways. On four occasions she chooses for the "Gospel" in the Mass, passages which relate to St. John the Baptist and his work of preparation. If we would prepare well for the coming of our King, we cannot do better than meditate on St. John the Baptist and try in our small measure to prepare as he did.

Point I.
The Preparation Before His Birth.

(1) *A prophecy.* Four hundred years before the Precursor's birth, Malachias prophesied of him: "Behold I send My angel," that is My *messenger*; and Our Lord tells us expressly (His words are noted by three of the Evangelists, St. Matthew, St. Mark and St. Luke) that this messenger was John the Baptist, who was sent by God to prepare the ways of the Messias.

(2) *His miraculous conception*—for his parents were both "well advanced in years." Both his father and mother were "just before God walking in all the commandments and justifications of the Lord without blame;" and they had their cross to bear—the "reproach" of having no son and therefore no hope of the Messias being born to them; but this did not prevent them from praying, as all fervent Israelites prayed, for the coming of the Messias. The answer to their prayer was nearer than they thought. One day as Zachary was performing the most solemn part of his priestly office—offering incense on the golden altar that stood "over against the veil" which separated the Holy Place from the Holy of Holies—he saw an angel standing on the right side of the altar, who, after he had calmed his fear, told him that his prayer was heard, that the Messias was coming, and that his wife Elizabeth was to bear him a son who was to be His Precursor, "he shall go before Him." The angel then prophesied many things about this child, which all show how careful was God's preparation of His Precursor:

> "Thou shall call his name John" (the Grace of
> God). Only those who had an important future

before them were named by God Himself before their birth.

"Many shall rejoice in his nativity." Many—both angels and men.

"He shall be great before the Lord." Great in sanctity and great in office.

He "shall drink no wine nor strong drink." He shall be a Nazarite, one separated and consecrated to God by a vow.

"He shall be filled with the Holy Ghost even from his mother's womb"—that is, he shall be cleansed from the stain of original sin and put into the state of grace before his birth as was Jeremias (Jer. 1: 5).

"He shall convert many" by preaching penance and telling of Him who takes away sin.

"He shall go before Him ... to prepare unto the Lord a perfect people." Zachary listened but he could not believe that what he heard was true, though Gabriel, who stands before God, had been sent expressly to him with the message of good tidings. He asked for a sign and He received one which not only proved to him that God can do what He wills as He wills, but also that He expects His children to trust Him.

When at length Zachary appeared from behind the curtain to the waiting and wondering people, instead of giving them the accustomed blessing (Num. 6: 24, 26), he made signs to them and remained dumb and they understood that he had seen a vision. God dealt severely with Zachary because he was so closely bound up with the Advent of the Messias. He had to be taught, and we through him, that the least venial sin may hinder God's work and designs, and that if we would be His instruments used by Him for the preparation of the Coming of His Son, we must be absolutely faithful about little things, full of confidence in God, setting no limit to His power and never doubting His dealings with us.

(3) *He was filled with the Holy Ghost.* Six months later, Elizabeth who had been waiting in solitude and silence for God to fulfil His designs, received a visit from the Mother of God, and the Precursor and the Messias Who was to come were brought into close contact. We cannot doubt that it was at that moment when, as Elizabeth said "the infant in my womb leaped for joy," that John was "filled with the Holy Ghost." Thus God cleansed His Precursor before his birth from the stain of original sin, again showing us that those who are to prepare for the Coming of His Son must be distinguished by their purity.

(4) *By the holiness of his mother and his home.* His mother taught by the Holy Spirit was the first to recognize Our Lady as the Mother of God; she was saluted by Our Lady and ministered to by her. She had the unspeakable privilege of having Our Lady with the blessed Fruit of her womb Jesus living under her roof for three months. A home where the Mother of God was welcomed and honoured—such was the home God chose for the Precursor of His Son.

POINT II.
THE PREPARATION AFTER HIS BIRTH.

"There was a man sent from God, whose name was John. This man came to bear witness of the Light, to prepare unto the Lord a perfect people." (The "Gradual" for the Vigil of St. John the Baptist). The Feast of the Nativity of St. John the Baptist is a Double of the First Class with an Octave, for Mary and her Son were present at his birth and he was "great before the Lord."

The eighth day was the day of circumcision and the naming day. Everybody naturally was calling him Zachary, but his mother who knew from her husband that the name was fixed, said: "Not so, but he shall be called John." They would not have it and appealed by signs to the deaf and dumb father, who wrote: "John *is* his name," for "he was so named of the angel before he was conceived." At that moment Zachary's penance came to an end and "he *spoke* blessing God." This fresh miracle was soon "noised abroad" and the people asked in fear: "What an one, think ye, shall this child be?" Zachary, "filled with the Holy Ghost," used his loosed tongue to sing his beautiful hymn of praise to God who had remembered His holy testament, and had allowed "the *Orient* from on high" to visit them. And then addressing his little son, he said: "And thou child shalt be called the prophet of the Highest, for thou shalt go before the face of the Lord to prepare His ways."

He began to "prepare His ways" by a life of hardship, solitude and penance, having no fixed home, living on what he could find in the deserts—locusts and wild honey, and wearing as a garment camels' hair with a leathern girdle. Tradition tells us he began all this at a very early age and he continued it "until the day of his manifestation to Israel," that is, until the day he left his solitude and began to preach—nearly thirty years later. He had thirty years' preparation for his life's work, like Him whose way he was preparing, and he was preparing it no less as a solitary in the deserts than as the great preacher of penance by the Jordan.

What lessons can we learn for our own preparation for the Coming of Christ this Advent?

1. That because we are going to be amongst those who in some way or other "prepare His ways," God has occupied Himself with our preparation even before we were born. Either by surrounding us with good, or by bringing good out of evil or by some of His many ways which are not our ways, He has had a hand in all that concerns us. We have first firmly to believe this, and secondly to co-operate with all God's designs for us, as John did.

2. That if we would prepare the ways of Christ we must be familiar with His Mother, accustomed to receiving her salutations and to returning them. That we must have her to live with us and take an interest in all that concerns us. Who could better help us to prepare for the Coming of her Son than His own Mother?

3. That we must be filled with the Holy Spirit and never turn Him out of our hearts by sin. It would be useless to try to prepare the way for Christ if we had not the co-operation of the Holy Spirit.

4. That penance in one form or another must have a share in our preparation for the Coming of Christ. All we know of John from the time of his infancy till he began his mission is that "he was in the deserts." It was not that he preferred such a life, but he felt that it was the one most suited to his own preparation for the Messias, for during those long years in the deserts he was preparing the way of Christ in his own heart; during

43

his mission he prepared it in the hearts of others. Solitude, fasting, lack of ease and comfort, coarse clothing—these were the allies which John chose to aid him in his preparation for the Coming of the King, for His "Kingdom is not of this world" and "the weapons of our warfare are not carnal" (2 Cor. 10: 4). He was consecrated to God, and he separated himself from everything that might interfere with his entire consecration.

Colloquy.

(1) With God the Father Who has chosen me to prepare the ways of His Son.

(2) With Him Who is coming.

(3) With God the Holy Ghost Who is co-operating with me.

(4) With Our Lady who is ready to let me do all my work by her side. (Ecclus. 24: 30).

(5) With St. John the Baptist who will obtain for me, if I ask him, the spirit of penance.

Resolution. To examine myself today as to the place penance is having in my Advent, and if it has none, to fix at least *one* daily penitential act.

Spiritual Bouquet. "He was in the deserts."

— ❧ —

St. John The Baptist. (2)
His Mission.

"In those days cometh John the Baptist preaching in the desert of Judea.... preaching the baptism of penance unto remission of sins." (Matt. 3: 1. and Mark 1: 4).

1st. Prelude. John preaching and baptizing by the Jordan.

2nd. Prelude. Gratitude to the "Friend of the Bridegroom" for Pointing Him out to the Bride.

Point I.
The Prophet.

When John was about thirty years of age the "word of the Lord" (Luke 3: 2) reached him in his solitude, just as it had done all the prophets of old from Samuel down to Malachias, but since then, that is for a period of four hundred years, God had spoken through no prophet. As a result of this "word" the "Prophet of the Highest" came into all the country about the Jordan—a large area—and began his mission. His arrival made a great stir and the people flocked to see and hear him. There "went out to him Jerusalem and all Judea and all the country about Jordan." All classes went—publicans, soldiers, even the Pharisees and Sadducees, for if this man were really a prophet sent from God, it behoved *them* to know all about him. What did the multitudes see? A man wearing a "garment of camels' hair and a leathern girdle about his loins," whose food consisted of locusts and wild honey—a man as the Angel Gabriel had prophesied "in the spirit and power of Elias" (see 4 Kings 1: 8). What did they hear? A voice of one crying in the desert: "Prepare ye the way of the Lord, make straight His paths." (Matt. 3: 3). And what were their conclusions? That this was he who was spoken of by Isaias the prophet (verse 3), that he was "sent from God" (John 1: 6) and that he "came for a witness, to give testimony of the light" (John 1: 7). What light? The "Light of the world." John came to proclaim that the dawn which the world had been so long watching was on the Point of giving place to day, that the "Sun of justice" was even now rising with "health in His wings" for those that feared God's name, and that they must go forth to meet him (Mal. 4: 2).

I too must go forth. What am I going to do today which will prove to myself, to my Guardian Angel, to my Patron

Saint, to Mary my Mother and to Him Who is coming that I am preparing the way of the Lord?

POINT II.

HIS PREACHING.

John came "preaching the baptism of penance for the remission of sins" (Luke 3: 3). His voice was like that of a herald proclaiming a great event that was close at hand. "Do penance, for the kingdom of heaven is at hand" (Matt. 3: 2). The Messias is coming to set up His Kingdom. He Whom you have so long expected is close to you, prepare for Him. Then John told them shortly and explicitly how to prepare: (1) "To believe in Him Who was to come" (Acts 19: 4). (2) To repent of their sins and bring forth fruits worthy of penance such as fasting and self-denial (Mark 2: 18). (3) To confess their sins (Mark 1: 5). (4) To be baptized as a sign of hope that their sins had been forgiven. John's baptism could not wash away sin, for it was no sacrament, St. Paul, as well as St. Mark and St. Luke, called it the "Baptism of penance" (Acts 19: 4). It was a baptism which proclaimed to all that he who submitted to it acknowledged himself to be a sinner and a penitent.

John the Baptist was greatly in earnest, for the time was short; he spoke very plainly to those whom he noticed coming to be baptized out of curiosity or human respect without any repentance or intention of doing penance. He warned them of the wrath of God which would fall upon sinners who persisted in their sin, of the folly of thinking that all was well with them because they had Abraham for their father; he told them that every tree which did not yield good fruit would be cut down and cast into the fire, that He Who was coming and was even now so nigh would divide all people into two classes—the wheat and the chaff, and that the great winnowing fan was already in His Hand.

The people then began to feel uncomfortable and alarmed, and anxious to make sure that they were not going to be blown away as chaff, or burnt "with unquenchable fires" by the Mighty One Who was coming; and different classes began to ask John what they must do. His answers were singularly appropriate and confirmed the opinion that he was indeed a prophet. To the people generally he counselled charity, kindness and brotherly love as the best possible preparation; to the public tax-collectors, who grew rich on the sums that they demanded in excess of the fixed tax, that they should do nothing more than that which was appointed; to the soldiers, that they should avoid violence and calumny and be content with their pay (Luke 3: 10-14). He showed clearly by his straight and simple answers that the best way for us to prepare for Him Who is coming, is to look into our daily life and occupations and change anything and everything that we know He would find faulty.

POINT III.

HIS BAPTISM.

One after another the people made up their minds to change their evil lives and bad habits. They made their good resolutions and as a proof of their sorrow for the past and firm purpose of amendment for the future, they went into the Jordan confessing their sins, and John baptized them. He told them then that He Who was coming was mightier than himself, and that He would baptize them with the Holy Ghost and fire. "Then cometh Jesus from Galilee to the Jordan unto John to be baptized by him!" Where had He come from? Straight from His home, from Nazareth, from His Mother.

He had come to fulfil John's prophecy, to begin His public ministry to the people, and He would begin it by identifying Himself with them. They were sinners, coming to confess their sins and He would be numbered with the transgressors (Isaias 3: 12). "But John stayed Him, saying: I ought to be baptized by Thee, and comest Thou to me?" (Matt. 3: 14). Though they were cousins it is probable that they had not met since their early childhood. One had lived in the seclusion of Nazareth and the other in the seclusion of the desert. "I knew Him not," (John 1: 31, 33) John said. It was probably the fact of someone coming for the baptism of penance who had no sins to confess that made John suspect and then protest; but he could not resist the gentle, authoritative words: "Suffer it to be so now, for so it becometh Us to fulfil all justice." Then when He had gone out of the water John saw a wonderful sight—he described it himself: "I saw the Spirit coming down as a dove from Heaven and He remained upon Him; and I knew Him not, but He Who sent me to baptize with water said to me: He upon Whom thou shalt see the Spirit descending and remaining upon Him, He it is That baptizeth with the Holy Ghost. And I saw; and I gave testimony, that this is the Son of God." (John 1: 32-34). He knew Him now—there was no longer any doubt, no more time of waiting and preparation, He Who should come had come. God Himself Pointed Him out to the faithful Precursor—a voice from Heaven said: "This is My beloved Son in Whom I am well pleased" (Matt. 3: 17). What a reward for John after his life of solitude and penance and mortification—to be in close contact with the Son of God, to see the Holy Spirit in the form of a dove, and to hear the Voice of God the Father, and thus have the seal set to his mission! "And I saw; and I gave testimony."

And what have the waters of Jordan to say? That He, over Whose Sacred Head they closed, has, by the contact of His precious Body, sanctified them and all other waters and given them power, when they are in contact with His mystical Body to wash away sin. Jesus went down to John in the Jordan not to *receive* a gift, but to *impart* one. From henceforth the waters will bring forth abundantly and God will say of His new creation, as He did in the beginning, that it is good. All three Persons of the Blessed Trinity were present at this new creation, the Holy Spirit brooded over the face of the waters for this new baptism was the Baptism of the Holy Ghost, the Voice of the Lord was upon the waters (Ps. 28: 3), the Voice, that is, of the Father proclaiming that He was well pleased, not only with His "Beloved Son" but with this first act of His public ministry; for in Him He saw a countless multitude coming out of the sanctified water, and of each one He will say: "*This is My beloved son, in whom I am well pleased.*"

"O Almighty Eternal God, preside over the mysteries of Thy great mercy, preside over Thy sacraments and send forth the Spirit of adoption to regenerate the new people, whom the font of Baptism brings forth to Thee" (Prayer for the Blessing of the Font on Holy Saturday).

> *Colloquy.* "Grant we beseech Thee, Almighty God, that Thy servants may walk in the way of salvation; and by following the exhortation of Blessed John the Precursor may securely attain the possession of Him Whom He foretold, Our Lord Jesus Christ." (Collect for the Vigil of St. John the Baptist).

> *Resolution.* To "prepare His ways" today.

> *Spiritual Bouquet.* "Blessed John the Baptist ... pray to the Lord our God for us."

— ❧ —

St. John The Baptist. (3)
His Testimony.

"This man came for a witness to give witness of the Light, that all men might believe through Him." (John 1: 7).

1st. Prelude. "John stood and two of his disciples and beholding JESUS walking, he saith: Behold the Lamb of God." (verses 35, 36).

2nd. Prelude. Grace so to hear his testimony that we follow JESUS.

POINT I.
"THAT HE MAY BE MADE MANIFEST THEREFORE AM I COME" (VERSE 31).

This was all John wanted, all he cared about, it was his vocation, it was the Point of his long years of mortification, the reason for his preaching and baptism; he was a man of one idea—the Christ is coming, I must manifest Him to the people. This man came for a witness to give testimony of the Light (verse 7). When the people wondering asked him: Art thou the Christ? Art thou Elias? Art thou the prophet? his answer was: No, I am only a voice proclaiming His coming. I, He? Oh, no, I am not worthy to be His slave. He is the Light, the Light of the whole world. "I saw the Spirit coming down as a dove from Heaven and He remained upon Him.... And I saw; and I gave testimony that this is the *Son of God*" (verses 32-34).

Let me look at my preparation for His coming this Advent and see whether I am in any way following in the footsteps of the great Precursor. Can I be said to be a person of one idea—that of manifesting my Lord to others? When people want to make much of me and my work and ask who I am, is my one thought to turn their eyes from me to Him Who is coming? Am I really persuaded that I am only here to make Him manifest? *Is* He being made manifest to others through me? Do those with whom I come in contact leave me, with a greater knowledge of Him, with a greater desire for His coming, with more anxiety about the salvation of their souls and with more zeal for that of others? Do my words and deeds, does my very manner, speak to them of Him and make them think of Him? "Art thou the Christ?" In one sense, yes, for I am or ought to be another Christ (*alter Christus*), living His life, doing His work and representing Him in the world.

POINT II.

"Behold the Lamb of God."

This is He, behold Him! He is the Lamb of God. He it is to whom all the lambs that have been sacrificed Point; their blood could not wash away sin, but "behold Him who taketh away the sin of the world." You are sorry for your sins, you have confessed them and I have baptized you as a sign that they are forgiven, now there is One among you who takes them away. Behold the Lamb of God! This was what John said when he saw Jesus the day after His baptism; he said the same thing the next day when he saw Him walking by the Jordan; two of his disciples were with him, Andrew and John (probably), and when they saw their master Pointing to Jesus and saying: "Behold the Lamb of God!" they did what John meant them to do, they left their master and followed *Him*. How well had the faithful Precursor prepared the way in their hearts! How thoroughly he had done his work! How absolutely he had effaced himself! There was no doubt, no hesitation in the minds of his disciples, no wondering whether John would mind; "*they followed* Jesus," and John had the joy of seeing Jesus turn and speak to them: "What seek you?" And then the joy of hearing them call *Him* Master. "Master, where dwellest Thou?" "Come and see." Then the Friend of the Bridegroom saw the three going away together, and he knew that his mission had not been in vain, the Bride was beginning to join the Bridegroom.

POINT III.

"HE THAT HATH THE BRIDE IS THE BRIDEGROOM."

It was not for nothing that Andrew and John spent that day with JESUS. They told others what they had found: "We have found the Messias, which is being interpreted the Christ," and they brought their companions one by one to JESUS, with the result that very soon the Baptism of the Holy Ghost was taking place in the Jordan as well as the Baptism of Penance, and the people instructed by John left the less for the greater.

There were "busybodies," as St. Paul calls them (1 Tim. 5: 13), even in those days, people who could not let others alone, who could not understand the situation or pretended that they could not; they "came to John and said to him: Rabbi, He that was with thee beyond the Jordan, to Whom thou gavest testimony, behold He baptizeth and all men come to *Him*" (John 3: 26). They were words calculated to stir up jealousy and ill-feeling; but John was too humble and too great to be disturbed by them, his answer was character-istic: "You yourselves do bear me witness, that I said that I am not Christ, but that I am sent before Him. He that hath the Bride is the Bridegroom." There is the proof that all I have been telling you is true. He has the Bride, the people all go to Him, you see for yourselves that He *must* be the Bride-groom; "but the Friend of the Bridegroom, who standeth and heareth Him, rejoiceth with joy because of the Bridegroom's voice. This my joy therefore is fulfilled." It was enough for "the Friend of the Bridegroom" to hear His Master's voice.

The necessity for him and his preaching was fast passing away and he knew it. He had been for a time the great man, the popular preacher, the one every one talked about, whose advice everyone sought, now he must stand aside and see his disciples gather round another master, himself not in the group at all. It is a position most workers in God's vineyard find themselves in sooner or later, they have to give place to others, to watch others reaping the fruit of their labours, to see those whom they have taught going to other teachers, those who have sought their advice seeking it elsewhere. How do they bear this difficult situation? How am I going to bear it when my turn comes? Am I going to pose as a martyr, craving for and expecting every one's sympathy? Am I going to put difficulties in the way of those who succeed me, and make it hard for those to whom it has been my privilege to minister? Some are even jealous and show their displeasure by criticizing those who succeed them! What was John's attitude? All he wanted was his Master and His Will. He was the "Friend of the Bridegroom." He was satisfied to stand on one side, and his cup of joy was full when he heard his Master's Voice. "He must increase" in the minds of the people "and I must decrease." Let me learn a lesson from John the Baptist and make my sacrifice beforehand, remembering that nothing matters so long as I am the friend of the Bridegroom, can hear His Voice and see the souls I have tried to help following Him. These are joys, real joys, and they are perhaps never fully realized till the cool shade of the background is reached.

Point IV.
John's Testimony of Himself.

1. I am sent before Him (John 3: 28).
2. I am the voice (chap. 1: 23).

3. I baptize with water (verses 26, 31).

4. I am not worthy (verse 27).

5. I am come that He may be made manifest (verse 31).

6. I ought to be baptized by Thee (Matt. 3: 14).

7. I knew him not. (John 1: 31).

8. I saw the Spirit coming down ... and He remained upon Him (verse 32).

9. I saw (verse 34); (that is, I understood).

10. I gave testimony that this is the Son of God. (ibid.)

11. I am not the Christ (verse 20).

12. I must decrease (chap. 3: 30).

Colloquy with St. John the Baptist.

Resolution. To bear my testimony.

Spiritual Bouquet. "Behold the Lamb of God!"

— ⚜ —

St. John The Baptist. (4)
His Martyrdom.

"Herod the Tetrarch, when he was reproved by him for Herodias, his brother's wife, and for all the evils which Herod had done, he added this also above all, and shut up John in prison." (Luke 3: 19, 20).

1st. Prelude. John the Baptist in Prison.
2nd. Prelude. Grace to be faithful unto death.

POINT I.
JOHN IN PRISON.

John knew no fear where right was concerned. His duty was to make the paths straight for Him who was coming and it mattered little to him whether he rebuked the Pharisees and Sadducees at the Jordan or Herod in his palace. Herod, however, could not brook such plain speaking and he had (at first) a mind to put him to death (but) "he feared the people, because they esteemed him as a prophet" (Matt. 14: 5). Herodias also had "laid snares for him and was desirous to put him to death and could not" because of Herod who knowing that John was "a just and holy man" (afterwards) protected his life (Mark 6: 19, 20). So John was shut up in prison; Josephus tells us that it was at a place called Machaerus on the east of the Dead Sea where Herod had a castle.

Let us go and visit John in that lonely prison, where he was cast quite at the beginning of Christ's ministry. His long years of preparation in the desert, his fearless, outspoken preaching, his generosity and humility in giving place to his Master, his important office of Forerunner of the Messias, his vision of the Blessed Trinity—are they all to end thus? Is this how God treats His friends? Is this the reward for fidelity and loyalty? Yes, St. John would be the first to answer, these are ever God's ways, "He must increase, I must decrease." John had indeed been specially favoured and he was specially favoured in prison too. It is not everybody whom God can trust with a trial such as this. John was still preparing the ways of the Lord, no longer by an active life, but by a life of suffering, solitude and privation. His patience and his perfect submission to God's Will no doubt prepared the ways of Christ in the hearts of many.

If He is to increase, I *must* decrease, it is only natural. Yes, it is natural for the saints to reason like this, but what about me? I want to be a saint. I often perhaps ask God to make me one, perhaps I even tell Him to use any means He likes, not to spare me. Does not this solve many a problem? God is only taking me at my word; the beginning, the middle and the end of the process of saint-making is *humility*. "I must decrease," and if I ask to be a saint, He will give me the humiliations and the sufferings which alone can teach me humility and unite me to Himself. What then does it matter, if I have to suffer physically or morally, if a career of usefulness in His service is suddenly cut short, if I have to stand on one side and see the work I love and for which my whole life has been a preparation, being done by another, if those I have taught do not seem to understand, if my life is full of little things I dislike and which seem made to annoy me—all these and everything else that can possibly happen to me are the direct result of my God-given wish to be a saint. Let me ask St. John the Baptist for courage to continue my prayer this Advent and to accept joyfully for Him Who is coming all that it entails, saying, to myself when something seems to happen on purpose to annoy me: "This is to help to make me a saint," and then seeing to it that it does.

POINT II.

THE END.

Vengeance still rankled in the breast of Herodias for John had said to Herod: "It is not lawful for thee to have thy brother's wife." She laid her plans and awaited her opportunity; it came on Herod's birthday; he gave a supper for the princes and tribunes and chief men of Galilee, and she made her daughter come in and dance till they were all so pleased that Herod swore to the girl: "Whatsoever thou shalt ask I will give thee, though it be the half of my kingdom." Herodias knew Herod and expecting that this would happen had told her daughter to do nothing without consulting her. "What shall I ask?" she said to her mother, who replied without any hesitation: "The head of John the Baptist." Herodias was evidently afraid that the king would change his mind and that her wicked plans would after all fail, for she impressed upon her daughter the necessity of haste. The girl went back *immediately, with haste* to Herod, and said: "I will that *forth-with* thou give me in a dish the head of John the Baptist." Herod was very sorry, for he was interested in his prisoner, also he knew him to be "a just and holy man" (Mark 6: 20) and he hesitated before such a crime; but he had taken an oath and to break it before his guests would be inconsistent with his dignity, besides "he would not displease" the girl, so he acted at once as Herodias had bidden him: "he sent and beheaded John in the prison, and his head was brought in a dish, and it was given to the damsel, and she brought it to her mother."

"Faithful unto death."—"O Lord, Thou hast set on his head a crown of precious stones" ("Communion" for the feast of the Beheading of St. John the Baptist, August 29th).

"And his disciples came and took the body and buried it, and came and told Jesus," told the Bridegroom that His "friend" was dead. "Which when Jesus had heard, He retired from thence by a boat, into a desert place apart."

"Faithful unto death," I must be too, if my preparation this Advent is to be anything like that of St. John the Baptist. He died to self long before his cruel death in the prison; his whole life from the day he went into the desert as a little child was a living death: "As dying and behold we live" (2 Cor. 6: 9). This is how St. Paul describes the state of all those who "*will* live godly in Christ Jesus" (2 Tim. 3: 12). It is the death of "the old man," the death of self; the "I" must ever be decreasing, ever receiving the blows which will one day, probably not before the soul's last day on earth, cause its death. Such is the prospect I have before me, if I would copy John the Baptist and be faithful unto death. What is my consolation and strength? That Jesus knows and sympathizes. Not one of the blows which cost me so much, not one of the sufferings, not one hour of desolation or loneliness or temptation or misunderstanding or unkindness, or any of the many things which are conspiring together for the death of "the old man," are lost upon Him. He knows, He cares, He sympathizes and He is glad, for in proportion as the "I" is decreasing, *He* is increasing in my soul.

Colloquy

(1) With John in the prison.

(2) With Jesus in "a desert place apart."

Resolution. To be "faithful unto death" today.

Spiritual Bouquet. "I spoke of Thy testimonies before kings and I was not ashamed" ("Introit" for the Feast of the Beheading of St. John the Baptist).

— ❧ —

St. John The Baptist. (5) His Character.

"What went you out into the desert to see? A reed shaken with the wind? But what went you out to see? A man clothed in soft garments? Behold they that are in costly apparel and live delicately, are in the houses of kings. But what went you out to see? A prophet? Yea, I say to you, and more than a prophet, for ... among those that are born of women, there is not a greater prophet than John the Baptist. But he that is the lesser in the Kingdom of God, is greater than he." (Luke 7: 24-28).

1st. Prelude. Jesus talking to His disciples about John.
2nd. Prelude. Grace to stand by and listen and learn.

POINT I.
HIS HUMILITY.

One day when John was in prison his disciples came and told him that they had heard that Jesus was working a great many miracles and that His fame was spreading all through the country. At Capharnaum He had healed a centurion's servant, and at Naim He had raised a widow's son to life; and the people were all glorifying God and saying: "A great prophet is risen up among us, and God hath visited His people" (Luke 7). This news sounded like music in John's ears; it was just what he wanted; it was a proof that his life's work had not been in vain: "He *must* increase." The disciples however who brought the news did not take at all the same view of the case. They were not pleased that another should take the place of their master while he languished in prison. John knew that had they been quite sure that JESUS was the Messias, such thoughts could have had no place in their minds, and so to strengthen their faith he sent two of them to JESUS with the question: "Art thou He that art to come or look we for another?" hoping no doubt that they might see some miracles for themselves, or at any rate that personal contact with JESUS would clear away their doubts.

See the beautiful humility of John's character, there is no thought for himself; he is only anxious still to Point out the Lamb of God and to remove all obstacles from His path in the hearts of all; he is still the voice crying with no uncertain sound. It happened (not by chance) that just when the two disciples arrived many miracles were being worked by JESUS, and in answer to their question, which they were probably now rather ashamed to put, He said: "Go and relate to John what you have heard and seen;" and He added: "Blessed is he whosoever shall not be scandalized in Me." Surely after that the disciples could never again stumble in their faith, and it must have been with joy in their hearts that they told their master of all they had seen and heard.

POINT II.
CHRIST'S TESTIMONY OF JOHN.

When the messengers had gone, JESUS began to talk to the people about His faithful Precursor, whom they all knew so well. "What went you out in the desert to see?" He asked them. Was it "a reed shaken with the wind?" Was it "a man clothed in soft garments" and living delicately? Was it "a prophet?" On another occasion He spoke of him as "a burning and a shining light" (John 5: 35). What praise this was on the lips of the Master! The four Points He picked out are characteristics that He appreciates not only in John but in all who are preparing for His Coming. Let us see where we stand with regard to them.

1. *A determination of purpose.* "What went you out into the desert to see? A reed shaken with the wind?" No, but a man of one idea, and who pursued that idea through all difficulties and opposition and failure, not counting the cost. I want to copy John the Baptist. I want to prepare the way of the Lord in my heart, how shall I do it? Not by allowing myself to be a reed shaken with the wind, trying very hard for a day or two and then giving all up and saying it is no use; not by making good resolutions and then quietly dropping them because they have been broken. No, but by a steady, determined effort, in spite of many failures, to overcome in myself everything which I know will be a hindrance to my King pursuing His way in my soul. He is never disappointed by my failures; these are more than made up for directly I tell Him that I am sorry. What pains His loving Heart is cessation of effort, giving up the fight, running away from the enemy instead of standing up to be knocked down

again, if my Captain thus wills to give me another opportunity of meriting, and of practicing humility. Saints are not made by victories all along the line, but by repeated failures humbly and patiently accepted, with a firm determination that each failure shall be the *last*. But what is the use when I know I shall fail again? I do not know; I need not fall, it is my own fault if I do. To do less than have a firm determination about the future, would be to lay down my arms. Every effort made for God leaves me holier, and as long as I keep on trying I am making progress in the spiritual life, though I cannot see it.

2. *Self-sacrifice.* "But what went you out to see? A man clothed in soft garments? Behold they that are in costly apparel and live delicately are in the houses of kings." John prepared for the Coming of his King by a life of self-sacrifice, every day giving up for the sake of Him Who was coming all the things that were just as dear to his nature as they are to mine. What part is self-sacrifice taking in my preparation for my King this Advent? I have no need to go into the desert or live the life of a hermit. It is the little tiny acts of self-sacrifice known only to my King and me which are so pleasing to Him. It is wonderful what notice He takes of little things which are done out of love to Him. If we could promise Him a certain number of these little acts every day—perhaps six or ten, or even *one*—and mark them down to ensure their being remembered, it would be a preparation very precious in His sight. To do a hard thing just because it is hard, to keep silent when I could say something sarcastic or clever but not quite charitable, to bear little physical sufferings without letting everybody know about

them, to be cheerful and bright when I am feeling tired and moody, to accept all that happens to me as coming straight from God's Hands, especially all the little crosses that come to me through others—these are the things that will make me a saint and I cannot keep Advent or any other season better than by practicing them. Nothing is too small for my King to notice. Let me then be generous and give Him all I can, remembering that as long as the little act *costs* me something, it is sure to be acceptable to Him; "He must increase, I must decrease," and it is by self-sacrifice that this great work will slowly but surely be accomplished in my soul.

3. *Fidelity to duty.* "But what went you out to see? A prophet? Yea, I say to you, and more than a prophet for ... amongst those that are born of women, there is not a greater prophet than John the Baptist. But he that is the lesser in the kingdom of God is greater than he." John was more than a prophet, because he not only prophesied of Christ as so many other prophets had done, but he was the last of the prophets, the immediate Forerunner of the Messias. No office could be greater than this and no one else ever held it, it was unique and made John "more than a prophet." Nevertheless, Our Lord said: "He that is the lesser in the kingdom of God is greater than he"—*lesser* in holiness and in office, but *greater* in dignity and privilege, because he is a member of the Holy Catholic Church and a partaker of her Sacraments. Thanksgiving that I am a member of the Holy Catholic Church should often find a place in my heart, and especially during Advent when the Church begins again to spread out before me all the

treasures of her Liturgy and when my thoughts and meditations are centred round Him Who is coming to be incarnate for that Church, to die for it, to make a plan which will enable Him to be with it "all days, even to the consummation of the world" (Matt. 28: 20), and finally to judge it that He may "present it to Himself a glorious Church, not having spot or wrinkle, or any such thing but that it should be holy and without blemish." (Eph. 5: 27).

If my privileges are greater than those of St. John the Baptist, my responsibilities are greater also. As I think how faithfully he fulfilled one of the greatest offices ever entrusted to man, let me remember that I too have a special office given me to fulfil, and it is no less important for me to fulfil it faithfully, than it was for St. John. It may be that my office is a very lowly one, that I have only one talent, but Jesus is taking notice how I am trading with it. What have His messengers to say when He asks: "What went you out to see?" Let the season of Advent inspire me to be up and doing—faithful in that which is least, living as one who has to give an account of each talent, each occasion of merit, each opportunity of influencing another, each inspiration of grace.

4. *Light giving.* "He was a burning and a shining Light." This was the secret of John's greatness, of his humility, of his courage, of his zeal. His heart so burned with love for God and zeal for His service that it shone out on all with whom he came in contact.

Let me make one last examen on myself here. Do I feel sometimes that my influence on others is very small, that my light seems to be hidden under a bushel, that try as I will, I cannot make any impression? May it not be that I am thinking too much about the shining of the light and too little about the burning? The candle must *burn* before it can *shine*. If my heart is in constant touch with the Sacred Heart of JESUS it will burn with His love and zeal, and the shining will follow as a matter of course, I need not trouble about it; but if I allow anything to separate my heart from His, even ever so little, the fire in my heart will die down; there may be a little glow left, unless I leave it too long, but there is not enough to "shine before men." "What went you out to see?" What answer would those with whom I live, those who know me best, have to give?

Colloquy with JESUS and St. John the Baptist.

Resolution. To win the approval of JESUS today by the way in which I prepare for His Coming.

Spiritual Bouquet. "What went you out to see?"

— ❧ —

"Incarnatus Est"

Regem venturum Dominum venite adoremus. [Come let us adore the King our Lord Who is to come.]

1st. *Prelude.* Picture of the Annunciation.
2nd. *Prelude.* Grace to understand the mystery of the Incarnation.

POINT I.
VENITE ADOREMUS.

"Come let us adore the King our Lord Who is to come." These are the opening words of the Invitatory which the Church uses every day at Matins during the first fortnight of Advent. Let us turn then from the Precursor, who has taught us so many lessons, to JESUS Christ Himself. What is He doing during these months of waiting before Christmas? He, too, is preparing, preparing for the work for which He has already come into the world, although He is not yet manifest. John the Baptist has Pointed Him out to me: "Behold the Lamb of God!" Now I will do what his disciples did—leave "the Friend of the Bridegroom" for the Bridegroom Himself. He has become incarnate for me; it behoves me then to keep as close to Him as possible, to love Him with all my heart and to copy Him as far as I can. He is God and therefore there can be nothing imperfect about Him; from the first moment of the Word being made flesh in the womb of His Mother till "she brought forth her first-born Son" on Christmas day, His faculties, His reason, His intelligence, His sensibilities were all in a state of perfection; He knew the past, the present, and the future; and He, the Source of grace, was pouring forth grace on all around Him. Directly we understand this, we feel that we must draw near, not only to adore but to sympathize, to wonder, to love, to learn, to imitate. For those who understand the Incarnation, His work did not begin on Christmas Day, but on the Feast of the Annunciation, when Mary said: "Behold the handmaid of the Lord, be it done unto me according to Thy word." What happened at that moment? The Holy Ghost overshadowed her, the Body of Our Lord was formed from her pure blood, God created the human Soul to dwell in it, and by the act of the Incarnation that Soul and Body became the Soul and Body of the Word, the Second Person of the Blessed Trinity; Mary became the Mother of God and Gabriel worshipped before the Tabernacle of the Word made flesh.

Mary was the next to adore; Joseph, Elizabeth, John, Zachary followed, and there may have been other privileged ones to whom Our Lord Himself revealed His secret; but the world at large went on as usual—it "knew Him not." The same thing happens every day in our midst. When the priest with his God hidden on his breast passes on his way to give the Bread of Life to some sufferer, only a few privileged ones know the secret and offer their silent adoration. V*enite adoremus.*

POINT II.

DIVINE ADORATION.

It was a *new life* that Our Lord entered upon at the moment of the Incarnation. He had had His Divine Life from all eternity, but God had never before been man. He now for the first time could express Himself through a human body. God could adore with human lips, could love with a human heart, could suffer through human senses, could plan with a human intelligence, could reason with a human mind. The consequence of the union of the two natures was that the human nature was perfect, more than perfect—it was Divine, and God received at the moment of the Incarnation, the first perfect human act of adoration, the first perfect human act of love, of humility and of all the other virtues. The God-Man could adore perfectly, because being God He knew God and knew what adoration was fitting for God; it was God adoring God and yet it was a human act, the act of a man like ourselves. At that moment God received what He wanted from one of the human race. The first breath drawn by His Son Incarnate made it worth His while to have created man in spite of the Fall. He received not only reparation but all He expected from the human race when He first created it. He was satisfied, and would have been satisfied even if that first moment had also been His last on earth. The Incarnation would have done its work, the justice of God could have required no more—a human will was perfectly submissive to His Will, a human heart beat in unison with His, a human creature offered itself as a victim for the race: "Behold, I come to do Thy Will, O My God," I have desired it. (Ps. 39: 8, 9). God received at the moment of the Incarnation a higher act of worship than He had ever received from all the nine choirs of Angels, and that act was a *human* act. Did the Angels who fell understand this and was this the cause of their rebellion? It is true that this first moment of the Incarnation would have more than satisfied God, but it was not enough for the God-made-Man. He would go on, on even to the death of the cross, not to satisfy His Father's justice, but His own love, and to show to those whom by His Incarnation He had made His brethren to what lengths love can go. Every breath He drew was as perfect as the first—a perfect offering, a perfect act of adoration; every beat of His Heart until He said: "Father, into Thy Hands I commend My Spirit," was a perfect act of love; every act, every thought, every word perfect, because they were the acts, thoughts and words of *God*.

POINT III.
THE PRACTICAL CONCLUSION.

What have I to do with these sublime truths? Everything, for He was incarnate *for me*. What does it mean? It means that He is my Brother and that He is giving to God what God must have, but what I cannot give Him; and that all I have to do is to unite myself to Him and to offer my imperfect acts of adoration, love, humility with His perfect ones. He has given Himself to me, that I may give Him back to God—a perfect offering with which God will be entirely satisfied. My God, I cannot adore Thee as I should, though I desire to do so with my whole heart, but JESUS is there incarnate for me, He is adoring Thee perfectly for me, accept His adoration and mine with it. My God, I love Thee, but I cannot love Thee enough, I cannot love Thee as I ought, I cannot love Thee as Thou deservest to be loved, but JESUS is incarnate for me, He has a human Heart which is loving Thee *perfectly*; I put my heart inside His, accept His love and mine with it. My God, I want to be perfectly submissive, perfectly humble, a perfect victim, but great though my desires are, I cannot arrive at the perfection which Thou dost require. Oh, look upon my Brother incarnate for me, accept all His perfections; let me offer my little struggles and desires and efforts with all that He is doing, for is it not all for me? "*Through* Him and *with* Him and *in* Him."

Let me go to Nazareth to Mary; she will welcome me for she knows that He has become incarnate *for me*. The Angel has just left her to take back her *Fiat* to Heaven. I will take his place and on bended knees before that holy shrine where the new Life has just begun, I will meditate. Never before perhaps have I so felt the need of thanksgiving, of adoration, of wonder, of love. All I offer now and from henceforth must pass through Mary to her Son, Who will offer my gifts with His own to His Father.

Colloquy with God-Incarnate.

Resolution. To thank God often today for the Incarnation.

Spiritual Bouquet. "He was incarnate by the Holy Ghost of the Virgin Mary and was made Man."

— ❦ —

"Ex Maria Virgine"

"Apud me est fons vitae." [*In me is the Source of life.*]

1st. Prelude. Mary, just after the Angel had departed from her.
2nd. Prelude. Grace to understand Mary's part in the Incarnation.

POINT I.

Mary Shares All With Her Son.

All the joy that the Incarnation brought to the Blessed Trinity, Mary to a great extent must have shared. There was the joy of God the Father, because He saw His designs in creating man fulfilled, His justice satisfied and a human creature doing Him perfect homage and bringing Him so much glory. There was the joy of God the Son, because at last He was united to our human nature, because He being God had nevertheless a human Soul and a human Body, to which He could unite all the Divine perfections, and by means of which He could carry out all His Father's designs for the lost human race. There was the joy of the Holy Spirit Who had overshadowed Mary and by His Divine power created in her a Soul and a Body so beautiful that they were worthy to be taken by the Eternal Word and for ever united to the Divinity. The Holy Ghost saw now a human Soul into which He could pour *all* the grace that would be needed by the whole human race. Of His fulness all were to receive (John 1: 16).

And what was the means whereby all this joy was given to the Blessed Trinity? The Body which had been formed from the most pure flesh and blood of Mary. She had lent herself at God's request to be the instrument used, and now she was the Tabernacle where the God-Man lay hidden. As He shared His life with His Mother, since it was her blood which was coursing through His Veins, so He shared all His acts with her. That first perfect act of adoration made by a human Soul to God was shared by Mary—she adored too. That first whole-hearted oblation of a human Soul to God was shared by Mary when she said her: *"Fiat mihi secundum verbum Tuum."* That first perfect act of love from a human Heart was shared by Mary for how close was the union between

69

Courtesy of *Campion Missal and Hymnal*

the Sacred Heart of JESUS and the most pure heart of Mary! When JESUS made acts of reparation of humility, of conformity to His Father's Will, Mary made them too—she could not but do so, for her life was so closely bound up with that of her Son; He became the mainspring of all she did. It was the charity and humility in *His* Heart that made her go to visit her cousin Elizabeth and make herself her handmaid; it was *His* salutation that made hers so powerful with regard both to Elizabeth and to the infant John; it was the thanksgiving in *His* Heart which overflowed into hers and made her sing her *Magnificat*. That Mary spent the nine months in adoration we may well believe, but she spent them also in union with her Son, sharing all with Him and giving us a perfect model of the interior life—which means not only that God shares in the acts of the soul, but also that the soul shares in the acts of God, Emmanuel—God with us—in order that we may be "with the King for *His* works" (1 Paralip. 4: 23).

POINT II.

MARY MY EXAMPLE.

He was incarnate for me, and His Mother is my Mother; it is to her that I must look now to teach me how to spend these days before His birth. Teach me, my Mother, to follow the great example which you set. Teach me, too, to rejoice in the wonders of the Incarnation. Who should be more filled with joy than I for whom He was incarnate? Teach me what the interior life means, teach me to allow Him to be the mainspring within me of all I do, so that the life which I live is not mine but His, the words which I speak not mine but His,—JESUS acting, thinking, speaking through me. This is the interior life which Mary understood so well and lived so perfectly during her time of waiting. There is, however, another side to the interior life, and this is the one we want to meditate about more especially, while we are thinking of the Son of God incarnate in the womb of the Blessed Virgin. He has taken human nature, my nature, and joined it to the Godhead. He has made Himself a partaker of my human nature in order that I may be a partaker of His divine nature. I must not only think, then, of His working in and through me, but of my working in and through Him. Mary entered into and shared not only His Acts of adoration and love and praise, but also the work He had come to do, His plans for the Redemption of the world. "They dwelt with the King for His works, and they abode there" (1 Paral. 4: 23). How true this was of Mary! It is in this that I must try to copy her. "I will abide in the Tabernacle of the Most High," and I will offer myself for *His works*, His interests shall be mine, He shall feel that *one* soul at least, sympathizes and cares and intends to co-operate in the great work He has come to do.

Let me, then, as the season of Advent is fast passing, ask myself once again: Am I doing all I can for the spread of the Kingdom which He came to this earth to set up? Am I trying to look at the world with the eyes of love with which He regarded it, when He first made Himself incarnate for it? Am I helping His poor, tending His sick, instructing His ignorant, bringing Home His sheep, loving His little ones, comforting His sorrowful ones? Such are "His works," and if I would do them, I must dwell with the King and learn to do them in His way—I must live an interior life.

POINT III.
ALL PASSES THROUGH MARY.

It is only those who do not understand the Incarnation who stumble over this statement. What could be more natural? If He chose to redeem the world through Mary, to do all His great works which depend on the Incarnation—such as the foundation of the Church with all her Sacraments—through Mary, is it strange that when I want to help the King in His works, I should do the same and put my little gifts for the King into her hands? Rather would it be strange if I wanted to work on a different plan from my King's. She is the *Janua coeli, the Turris Davidica, the Sacrarium Spiritus Sancti*; the Tabernacle where He was incarnate for me. Through her and by means of her, He hands me all the graces I receive. What more natural than that I should make use of such a messenger to take back my offerings? And do they lose in the transaction? Surely they must gain, first because she will purify them and add to them her own merits and graces, and secondly because a gift presented by His own Mother cannot but be enhanced in value.

Blessed Grignon de Montfort says: "God has chosen her for the treasurer, steward and dispenser of all His graces, so that all His graces and all His gifts pass through her hands; and according to the power she has received over them, as St. Bernardine teaches, she gives to whom she wills, as she likes, and as much as she likes, the graces of the Eternal Father, the virtues of Jesus Christ and the gifts of the Holy Ghost." We may, if we like, "do all our actions with Mary, in Mary, by Mary, for Mary, in order to do them more perfectly with Jesus, in Jesus, by Jesus, and for Jesus, our Last End."[1]

If I am a child of Mary in anything more than in name, I shall not hesitate to use this great privilege which is offered to me, knowing that by so doing, not only will the value of my prayers and penances and actions be enhanced in God's sight, but my merits and graces will be increased. Mary will

1 *"The Secret of Mary unveiled to the devout soul"* by Louis-Marie Grignon de Montfort

see to it that her children who thus trust her have a Benjamin's portion.

Colloquy with Mary, asking her to obtain for me during this waiting time the grace to trust her with all my secrets for her Son.

Resolution. To dwell "with the King for His works" today.

Spiritual Bouquet. Janua coeli, ora pro nobis.

— ❦ —

"The Lord Is Nigh"

"Brethren, rejoice in the Lord always; again, I say rejoice. Let your modesty be known to all men. The Lord is nigh. Be nothing solicitous; but in everything by prayer and supplication with thanksgiving let your petitions be made known to God. And the peace of God which surpasseth all understanding, keep your hearts and minds in Christ Jesus." (Phil. 4: 4-7). (The "Epistle" for the Third Sunday of Advent).

> *1st. Prelude.* Before the Tabernacle.
> *2nd. Prelude.* Grace to remember the Presence of God.

The Lord is nigh because by His grace He is within us, because by His omnipresence He is "not far from every one of us" (Acts 17: 27), because in the Blessed Sacrament He is with us "all days, even to the consummation of the world" (Matt. 28: 20) and because it may be *today* that He will come in judgment. In consequence of this nearness of our God to us, from whatever Point of view we regard it, St. Paul tells us that there are certain practices which are incumbent upon us.

Point I.
"Rejoice in the Lord Always."

To rejoice *always*—this is my duty, because the Lord is nigh. When joy is absent from me, it is because faith in His nearness is absent. When clouds hide the Sun of Justice, and I am disposed to be sad and despondent, let me make an Act of Faith in His Presence: My God, I know that Thou art within my soul, because I have reason to believe that I am in the state of grace. My Jesus, I believe that Thou art there in the Tabernacle. My God, I believe that Thou art truly present behind every person and every circumstance and every trial. My Jesus, I believe that it may be today that Thou wilt summon me to stand before Thee as my Judge.... I shall find that Acts of Faith, such as these, will help to dispel the despondency and send me on my way rejoicing. How can I do anything but rejoice when I think of the Divine Inhabitation? Can I be sad when I realize the presence of Jesus in the Blessed Sacrament of the Altar and all that means to me? Can I allow circumstances and trials to depress and crush me when I know with what infinite love and care they have been arranged for me by Him who hides *Himself* in each one of them? And if the thought that the Lord is nigh in judgment can hardly in itself be a thought that brings joy, yet, when I know how much value He sets on joy, I should like Him to find me rejoicing when He pays that always unexpected visit to my soul. The Lord is nigh, therefore *rejoice*. To rejoice *in the Lord* is always possible, it only means a realization of the supernatural, and as soon as that is realized, everything is seen in a different light. "In Thy light we shall see light" (Ps. 35: 10), and "at Thy right hand are delights even to the end" (Ps. 15: 11). It is just because the Lord is nigh that I cannot but rejoice, and it is only when I forget His Presence that the clouds have the power to chill and depress me and rob me of my joy. St. Paul is afraid that I *may* forget, and so he adds: "*Again* I say: Rejoice."

POINT II.

"LET YOUR MODESTY BE KNOWN TO ALL MEN."

The Greek word which is translated "modesty" means more, it means fairness, kindness, gentleness, moderation, self-restraint, not insisting on strict justice. These are the qualities by which I am to be known to all men, *because* the Lord is nigh. He is within me—always if I will by His grace and often by the Blessed Sacrament. I may truly be said to "bear God in my body." What follows? I am His representative to the world; He is living His life in the world through me; if people want to know something about God and what He is like, they ought to be able to find out by watching my life.

The Lord is nigh—my gentleness has to recall this fact to others. "The servant of the Lord must not wrangle, but be mild towards all men." (2 Tim. 2: 24). He must not stand up for his rights, though strictly speaking he may have them; he must not be wedded to his own opinions and ever anxious to give them; he must not argue and strive to show that he is in the right, which means that everybody else is in the wrong. No, if he does these things, he is giving an altogether false representation of Christ Who is within him, of the Lord Who is so nigh.

Some people are gentle by nature, but it is not this natural quality of gentleness, often a mark of weakness of character and will, which is to be known to all men. It needs a strong will and much self-restraint to show the gentleness of Christ; it means the temper kept in check when slighting, insulting or unkind words are said; it means keeping silence when misjudged or falsely accused because "Jesus was silent;" it means keeping back the cutting word or the stinging sarcasm and letting them die away before His Presence; it means giving up a cherished plan or desire and letting no one except Him Who asks for the sacrifice know what it costs; it means being able to let a matter drop, though we may be in the right—such is the gentleness of Christ, which we have to make known so that by our behaviour others may be attracted to Him Who is so nigh. What a Point it would give to our preparation for His Coming this Advent, if each day found us striving to let our gentleness win others to Him and make them long to know the Babe of Bethlehem.

POINT III.

"Be Nothing Solicitous."

Take no thought, for your Heavenly Father knoweth that you have need. Do not be solicitous, careful, anxious about anything, there is no need for the Lord is nigh. He knows what is best for His child. He can alter things if He likes, leave all to Him. All worry and anxiety only come really from want of faith. Does a child worry when its father is near? No, it leaves everything to him without any care. The Lord is nigh, be nothing solicitous. The way may seem blocked, but it is not blocked to Him; the Lord is still nigh, "He knoweth my way" (Job 23: 10), is it not enough?

Let me love and trust and continually talk to Him Who is so near; let me remember that I am never alone, that the difficulties and problems and sorrows of life concern *two*, that the responsibility is *shared*, that the important business of life is a *joint* one. Surely with such a Partner, One who is never absent but always nigh, I need be in *nothing* solicitous.

POINT IV.
"IN EVERYTHING BY PRAYER AND SUPPLICATION WITH THANKSGIVING, LET YOUR PETITIONS BE MADE KNOWN UNTO GOD."

The conclusion I arrived at in the last Point is a just one, but I am not on that account to do nothing. He must have my active co-operation and whether I am working for my own salvation or for the salvation of others or, which ought to be the case, for both, I must in *everything* I do, let my petitions be made known unto God, that is, I must never act on my own responsibility. I am going to see such and such a person, come with me; I have this letter to write, tell me what to say; I have a difficult matter to settle, give me the necessary wisdom and tact; I am going to rest, or to take my food or my recreation, I want Thee with me all the same—such must be my requests. What about my mistakes, the things I forget and leave out, the faults that I mean with all my heart not to commit, but which I am always falling into all the same? Ah, it is here that the inestimable benefit of having such an all-powerful Partner comes in. Instead of bewailing my incapability, which only makes me still less capable, I must make my requests known to Him. What sort of requests will these be? I have committed that fault, made that same mistake again, please forgive me and correct it; I have forgotten to say something I meant to say, please say it for me; I have been stiff, unyielding, ungracious, discourteous, harsh, severe, please make up for my deficiencies and whatever happens do not let them judge Thee by Thy representative, make them understand that He for whom I am working is never anything but gracious and gentle, that He never breaks the bruised reed nor quenches the smoking flax; do not let me spoil Thy work. Such are the prayers and supplications by which I should continually be making known my needs to Him Who is always nigh.

And what about the thanksgiving? This is most necessary, otherwise, ashamed though I am to confess it, I shall be attributing the successes to my own powers and skill and capability! It seems hardly credible, but unfortunately past experience tells me that it is all too true. In order to guard against such a distorted and absurd view of things, St. Paul tells us not to forget the *Thanksgiving*. The Lord is nigh, let me turn to Him and say: *Deo gratias*, for it is He Who has prevented my awkwardness from spoiling His work. He loves to be thanked and He notices when He is not. Let me be thoroughly persuaded that the work *is* all His, and that if anything succeeds that *I* do, it is only because He has allowed *His* success to pass through me, thus thanksgiving will not only be easy but natural. But who is ever going to persuade me that no glory is due to me? "Who is sufficient for these things?" He Who condescends to be my Co-worker. He can do even that, if I love Him sufficiently to *want* Him to have all the glory.

POINT V.

THE RESULT—PEACE.

"The peace of God which passeth all understanding (shall) keep your hearts and minds in Christ JESUS." This will be the result, not of Our Lord being nigh, but of our *realization* of His nearness. A great peace will *keep*, that is, take possession of, our hearts and minds. Everything will be right because it comes straight from God's Hands. "*My* peace I give unto you, not as the world giveth do I give unto you" (John 14: 27). God's peace passes the understanding of the world, it has nothing to compare with it. It passes the understanding of God's children too. It is one of the mysteries with which He blesses His own and makes life possible for them in a world of turmoil.

Colloquy with Him Who is nigh.

Resolution. To remember that I am never alone.

Spiritual Bouquet. "The Lord is nigh."

— ❦ —

The Interior Life. (1)
Humility.

"I am Thy servant, I am Thy servant and the son of Thy   hand-maid." (Ps. 115: 16).

Janua coeli, ora pro nobis.

1st. *Prelude.* The Gate of Heaven.
2nd. *Prelude.* Grace to enter that gate and learn.

We are going now to keep very close to Mary. She is passing all these precious days in communion with her Son and He is teaching her what conformity to Himself means. But she has Him not for herself alone but for all those for whom He has made Himself incarnate and has come to die. The time passed within that "Gate of Heaven" was the first stage of His earthly journey and He was there for me, for my learning. He was already my Model. Let me go, then, today to the "Gate of Heaven," go to Mary and ask to be allowed to study some of those heavenly lessons which were so dear to her heart. *Janua coeli, ora pro nobis.* "Remember, O most gracious Virgin Mary, that never was it known that any who implored thy help or sought thy intercession were left unaided. Inspired with this confidence I fly unto thee.... O, Mother of the Word Incarnate despise not my petitions, but in thy mercy hear and answer me."

Point I.
The Humility of Jesus.

We cannot contemplate this stage of Our Lord's life without being struck first of all by the humility and self-abasement of it, by the way in which in some sense He *annihilated* Himself that He might do His Father's Will. St. Paul says: "He emptied Himself ... being made in the likeness of men" (Phil. 2: 7). He stripped Himself, robbed Himself of all that He possessed: *Semetipsum exinanivit.* We know that Mary, His created Home, was chaste and pure, that no breath of sin had ever touched her, that the Holy Spirit Himself had overshadowed her and had undertaken the preparation and the adornment of the earthly Tabernacle of the Word; but pure and holy though she was, Mary was only a creature and He was the Creator. He was God and she was one of the human race. His place was on the highest throne of Heaven and yet "He abhorred not the Virgin's womb" but there lived hidden from the sight of all, like any other infant and yet wholly unlike, because He had full possession of His faculties and intelligence. In the manger He will be *seen*, and so will be loved, pitied and worshipped; there will be many consolations which will go far to lessen and soften His humiliations, but *here*, He is alone, hidden; His very existence not even suspected. He has annihilated Himself, made Himself nothing. He could have taken our nature, had He so wished, without all these humiliations; why then did He despise not the Virgin's womb? Because this is to be His principle all through His life, He will love "unto the end." He will leave nothing undone that He could possibly do. He came to do His Father's Will and He will do it thoroughly. He will bear all the humiliations because He wants to be my Model and to teach me that there is only one way of learning humility.

POINT II.

THE HUMILITY OF MARY.

Mary, though she cannot see Him, is sharing intimately all His humiliations. She knows as no one else can all He is going through; and because she is His Mother she feels more intensely than anyone could what His humiliations are, she can never forget them. She shares all with Him and He lets her; her sympathy is His consolation. Of all the virtues of the interior life, humility is the one which is the most strongly marked in Mary, and perhaps more strongly during these nine months than at any other time. It was her humility which attracted the Eternal Word from Heaven to take up His dwelling in His earthly Tabernacle. It was her humility which made her visit her cousin Elizabeth. It was her humility which made her sing in her *Magnificat* of the great things God had done for her and how He had regarded the low estate of His handmaid. It was her humility which made her ready to suffer any humiliation rather than disclose God's secret to St. Joseph. It was her humility which made her incapable of resenting all the humiliations she had to bear at Bethlehem on Christmas Eve—and all this humility, all this power to bear humiliations, came from the fact that she was living an interior life, living a hidden life with her Son, looking at everything from His Point of view and not from her own.

POINT III.

"LEARN OF ME."

Now let me turn from the interior life of JESUS and Mary to my own. JESUS lived His interior life for me. If He allowed

Mary to share it, He will allow me, for He said once that He counted as His Mother all those who do His Will. His Will is quite clear: "Learn of me for I am *humble*." Dare I go to the "Gate of Heaven" and say that I want to learn to be humble, that is, that I want to copy JESUS and Mary in their humiliations? It takes a great deal of courage to ask for humiliations, and perhaps it is almost impossible to do so without some pride lurking in the request; but what I can do is to be so anxious to learn to be humble as He bids me, that I ask for strength to bear the humiliations that He sends. How *do* I bear them? Do I say: Oh well, it is a humiliation, I must bear it! or, Oh well, I shall never learn humility without humiliations! or: I am always getting humiliations, some people are, but I gladly accept them! All such speeches have their source, not in humility but in pride. Can we imagine Mary talking like this? Humiliations will never do their blessed work of making me humble if I thus use them to attract attention to my supposed virtue. A humiliation is spoiled the moment it sees the light; it has no strength left in it wherewith to produce humility. Do I want to be humble? Then let me go to that quiet retreat where JESUS is humiliating Himself for me, let me take all my humiliations there. When I am left out, forgotten, despised, when my help is unasked, my opinion disregarded, when things are said of me that are hard to bear, when reflections are made on my actions, let me go at once to where JESUS is hidden and hide myself and my pain there, my one fear being lest anyone but He should suspect my pain, and this not from stoicism or natural self-restraint, so pleasing and consoling to self, but because I am afraid of spoiling my chance and preventing the humiliation from doing its work. If I can only deposit it safely in His Heart before another sees it and robs me of my jewel, all will be well. He who suffered all those humiliations for me, will know how to ease my pain, He will tell me what a consolation it is to Him that His child understands and is trying to make a faithful copy.

Colloquy. O Mary, "Gate of Heaven" keep the gate wide open and beckon me in whenever you see me in danger of falling through my pride. You know the dangerous moments, please forestall them for me, and when I am safe, and listening to the Sacred Heart beating for me, the pain of the humiliation will be turned into joy and perhaps I shall make Him feel that His humiliations have not been in vain.

Resolution. To examine myself today on how I take my humiliations and to resolve how I will take them for the future.

Spiritual Bouquet. "Learn of Me for I am humble."

— ❦ —

The Interior Life. (2)
Oblation.

"Sacrifice and oblation Thou wouldest not, but a Body Thou hast fitted to Me. Holocausts for sin did not please Thee. Then said I: Behold I come. In the head of the book it is written of Me, that I should do Thy Will, O God." (Heb. 10: 5-7).

1st. *Prelude.* "Thy holy Tabernacle, which Thou hast prepared from the beginning" (Wisdom 9: 8).

2nd. *Prelude.* Grace to be generous.

Point I.
The Oblation of Jesus.

As soon as the Word had taken possession of His earthly home, He began to live His new life—a life in all its fulness of knowledge and of grace and which will ever remain at its highest Point, a life of infinite worth, a life lived for others, a life abounding in merits and satisfactions, a life of contemplation and yet of activity, a life to be studied carefully by all who seek to live an interior life and specially by those who for the love of their Incarnate God hide themselves in the cloister.

This new life was before everything else a life of *oblation*. The first act of the Word Incarnate was to offer Himself to His Father: Here I am; I have come to do Thy Will and I have come to do it not for Myself but for all creation; I offer Myself to do what it cannot do and to satisfy Thy claims. He made Himself, then, from the first moment of His existence a *Victim*—a Victim laid on the altar. This was His first posture, and He will keep it not only during this first stage of His life, but all through His life and all through His Sacramental life, whether the Host is offered to God at the Holy Mass or is living Its life of a Victim in the Tabernacle; and in Heaven He will still be "the Lamb as it had been slain."

With the oblation of Himself, so acceptable to the Father, the Victim offers all that concerns Him, all for which He has come to this earth, all His designs for man's salvation. He submits all His plans for His great building, the Holy Catholic Church, of which He offers Himself to be the Chief Cornerstone, dwelling in it as its life throughout all time. He offers Himself also to bear all the effects of His oblation and to drink the chalice to the dregs. He offers Himself as a Surety for the whole human race and for it He offers all His merits and satisfactions. He keeps nothing back—the whole of the life just begun is offered for the glory of God and the salvation of the world. It is a whole burnt-offering, a holocaust offered at its very beginning to Him Who "spared not even His own Son, but delivered Him up for us all." (Rom. 8: 32).

POINT II.

THE OBLATION OF MARY.

Mary lived her life with her Son and to her He communicated His secrets. It is impossible to imagine that He did not reveal to her His plans and designs which were the reason of His coming to this earth, and how He was going to carry them out. She knew, then, that she was the Mother of a Victim; and when He offered Himself to God, she joined in, offering herself and her Son for all that He wished. "Behold the handmaid of the Lord!" Here I am, I offer myself to Thee, do what Thou wilt with me. This was Mary's attitude all through her life from the time when her *Fiat* was a sign for the Incarnation to take place, till she stood on Calvary's Hill assisting at the offering of the Victim. Truly had the Mother of Sorrows caught the spirit of her Son; all through her life she regarded Him as a Victim. When He was forty days old she formally offered Him to God, and her life though bound up with His was nevertheless detached from Him, as from something given to another. Now at this early stage of His life, Mary is learning her lesson and gaining her strength. She is doing it by leading an interior life, hidden with her Son.

O my Mother, as I come today to the holy Tabernacle "prepared from the beginning" where the Sacred Victim lies hidden, help me to make my life one with His as thou didst, help me to detach myself from everything for His sake and to say my *Fiat* whenever He asks for it.

POINT III.
LEARN OF ME.

If I want to live an interior life, I must model it on the life of JESUS hidden in the womb of His Mother. He wants me to lead it for He is ever saying: Learn of Me Who led this life for you. An interior life must be essentially a life of oblation. This is its foundation: the offering of the soul as a holocaust to God and then regarding itself as a victim, all it has and does and is and thinks and plans, belonging not to itself but to God. It lies on the altar waiting to be consumed; it is not surprised when it is treated as a victim and feels the flames, not surprised, that is, when it is forgotten and thought nothing of; its life is *hidden*, how should people remember it! If it has to suffer, it considers it the most natural thing in the world for a victim. If its plans are all frustrated, it knows that it is lying there on the altar to do God's Will, not its own, and that this is only the fire consuming the victim; if it did *not* happen thus the victim might indeed be surprised and anxious, wondering whether God had accepted its sacrifice. "Present your bodies a living sacrifice, holy, pleasing unto God, your reasonable service" (Rom. 12: 1). The sacrifice is ever *living*, and ever being consumed. The victim feels keenly all the many processes by which God shows that He has accepted the offering, but if it copies its Model, there will be no complaint, no drawing back of the offering, no wishing that it had chosen an easier course, no wondering whether it had made a mistake in its vocation; rather will there be joy in its heart because in its humble way it is like its Master, and each fresh touch of the fire will be to it a fresh proof that God has not forgotten it, but has taken it at its word and counts on it to be all that it promised to be. What is necessary for all this? Only one thing: *Love*. If I love, I can do it. "Walk in love as Christ also hath loved us and given Himself an oblation for us."

O my little JESUS, hidden there for me and offering Thyself for me, teach me to be generous, teach me to love Thee as Thou deservest; help me to lie quietly and unresistingly on the altar. I am not alone. Thou art there, bearing all with me and giving me the necessary strength to bear all for Thee. Help me to sacrifice willingly all my cherished desires and tastes, all my will. Thou didst withhold nothing from me, help me to withhold nothing from Thee. So shall I make Thee some reparation for all the time wasted in the past, for all the sins committed against Thy love; so only can I obey Thy command: "Learn of Me," and make some little return for Thy infinite love.

Colloquy with JESUS and His blessed Mother.

Resolution. To offer myself as a victim today.

Spiritual Bouquet. "Walk in love as Christ also hath loved us, and hath delivered Himself for us, an oblation and a sacrifice to God." (Eph. 5: 2).

— ❧ —

The Interior Life. (3) Imprisonment.

"I was in prison and you came to Me." "Lord when did we see Thee ... in prison?" (Matt. 25: 36, 39).

1st. Prelude. Turris Davidica.
2nd. Prelude. Grace to visit Him in His prison.

POINT I.

DEPENDENCE.

Our blessed Lord's life, during the nine months, was a life of imprisonment. He chose for Himself a position of dependence, helplessness and inability. He Who was the Light of the world chose to live in darkness; He Whom the Heavens cannot contain chose a more cramped position than any prisoner has ever had to endure; He Who was infinite allowed Himself to be confined; He Who was immortal took a mortal body. He endured all the sufferings that helplessness and inability and immobility entail; and we have to keep reminding ourselves that He was fully alive to all His sufferings. We are not making an imaginary picture, but trying to realize what were the actual facts of those nine months. His Mother understood, let us try to do the same. Let us go to the "Tower of David" where Our Lord is kept a prisoner and let us remember that He is there for us. Let us not be amongst those to whom He will have to say sadly: "I was in prison and you did not visit Me." Later on, at the end of His life, He will allow His own people to take Him prisoner and will stand still while they put the chains on His wrists and will allow Himself to be dragged where they wish. Later on still He will choose to be imprisoned in the little Host and to make Himself to the end of time our Prisoner of Love.

Thy imprisonments were all voluntary, my JESUS, they were all suffered out of love and out of love for me. Oh, may these visits that I am paying Thee during the blessed season of Advent result in my imbibing more of the spirit of my imprisoned Master. Mine too is a voluntary imprisonment; I am His captive because I said: I will be His servant, "I will not go out free" (Ex. 21: 5). I gave up my liberty, preferring to be His prisoner rather than the devil's free man. Naturally He takes me at my word, but oh, sometimes prison-life is very hard to bear! He chains me to a bed of sickness, where I must lie still and see the work I long to do left undone or, what is perhaps harder still, badly done; He gives me great desires and no means of fulfilling them; He fills me with plans and schemes for His glory and then seems to make it impossible for them to be realized; He trains me, as I think, for some particular position and then detains me in another for which it seems to me I have not the least aptitude; He sets limits to my strength; He seems to keep me always in the background; He appears to use everybody else except me for His work; He seems to cramp my efforts and allow me no scope for the talents He has given me.

The Divine Prisoner Himself answers my plaints: My child, all these things only prove that you are My prisoner, that I have taken you at your word and that I do with you as I wish. Your time is not lost any more than Mine was. By doing My Will, however inscrutable it may seem to you, you are doing far more for Me than if you were doing your own. Trust me, be patient, bear and suffer all for Me, Who am a Prisoner for you. I love you to be dependent on Me, I love you to walk by faith, I love you to trust Me, and so I am constantly doing little things to remind you that you are My prisoner. Strive to be a prisoner of love as I am, that is (1) one who is in prison for love of another, (2) one who loves his chains, (3) one whose every act in prison is done to please Me.

POINT II.

DARKNESS.

How much darkness adds to the sufferings of prison life! It was a suffering which JESUS living in Mary endured for me; and yet while He, the Light of the world was there, her blessed womb was flooded with light, with the light of Heaven itself.

What light this thought throws on my interior life! The suffering of darkness! It is a suffering which He inflicts upon many of His prisoners of love. "Who is there among you that feareth the Lord, that heareth the voice of His servant, that

90

hath walked in darkness and hath no light? Let him hope in the name of the Lord and lean upon his God." (Is. 50: 10). If only I can make myself believe that the darkness is permitted by Him there will be a ray of light at once in the darkness because God is there, "Surely God is in this place." But how can I be sure that the darkness is permitted by Him? If I am living the interior life, if my intention is to please Him in all that I do, and if, however badly I succeed, I never willingly take back that intention, then *I am pleasing God*; and if I am pleasing God, I am one of His own dear children, just as really as was His Son Who did always the things that pleased Him. If I am one of His children I know, for He has told me so, that *nothing* can happen to me without His knowledge and His permission, yea His arranging. So if I have to walk in darkness rather than in light, if desolation is my spiritual lot and consolation is almost unknown to me, if a veil hides God's face and my continual cry is: "Oh, that I might know and find Him" (Job 23: 3), if prayer seems impossible, if I have a distaste, almost a repugnance for all spiritual things, if even Our Lady seems to desert me, if at times I am on the brink of despair, tempted even to think that my soul will be lost, if, in short, darkness, thick darkness has settled down on my soul—what then? "Let him *hope* in the name of the Lord and lean upon his God." But how can I hope in darkness, how can I lean upon Someone Who is not there? By faith, that is by saying all the time: This darkness is *His* doing, therefore it is what He wants for me. "I, the Lord create darkness!" That makes all the difference.

Faith, as it always does, lets a streak of light into the darkness; God is there and it is only to make the soul more sure of this that He permits the darkness. If the soul can find and recognize God in the darkness then it knows Him very intimately and this is what God wants—a love so great that it detects the Beloved One at once. Does darkness make any difference to the intercourse of those who love? They rather prefer it, so that all may be shut out except each other. This is what God wants from those whom He is teaching to be interior—He puts them into prison and leaves them in the dark. Are they going to be unhappy, to repine and complain, longing for consolation and all the sweet things with which God fed them when they hardly knew Him? Not if they have faith; and if their faith is strong, they will hardly be able to distinguish desolation from consolation, God's absence from His presence, yea the very darkness itself from the light! For is it not their God who is the cause of all that is happening to them, and is not that enough for those who love? They only want His Will, not their own, and His Will is to keep them in prison and in the dark and so to unite them more closely to Himself Who for their sake faced for nine months the darkness of the womb. In the terrible moments when despair seems so near us, let us hold on to the fact that we *want* to please God and therefore that we are His children and that He loves us and is arranging everything—this is the little ray of hope in the darkness, the line of light, and in it we read the words: "I give them life everlasting and they shall not perish for ever; and no man shall pluck them out of My Hand." (John 10: 28).

Colloquy with JESUS, the Light of the world, imprisoned in darkness for me.

Resolution. To lean upon my God in times of darkness.

Spiritual Bouquet. "I form the light and create darkness." (Is. 45: 7).

— ❧ —

The Interior Life. (4) Hiddenness.

"Verily, Thou art a hidden God, the God of Israel the Saviour." (Is. 45: 15).

1st. Prelude. Jesus hidden in Mary.
2nd. Prelude. Grace so to find Him that I may live the hidden life.

Point I.
"Thou Art a Hidden God."

He was hidden in the womb of His Mother; all through His life and death on earth, His Divinity was hidden except to a very few; in His Eucharistic life He will hide Himself to the end of time in the little Host. He seemed to love hiding when He was on earth and when He did reveal Himself, it was something like a child playing at hide and seek. He hid Himself from the Samaritan woman till He had heard all her story and then said suddenly: "I am He (the Messias) Who am speaking with thee" (John 4: 26). The blind man whom He cured had not the least idea Who He was till Jesus, hearing that he had been reviled and cast out of the Synagogue, went and talked to him about the Son of God and then said in the middle of the conversation: "Thou hast both seen Him, and it is He that talketh with thee" (chap. 9: 37). From Mary Magdalen at the sepulchre He deliberately hid Himself under the form of a gardener that He might have the joy of suddenly surprising her with His presence. Perhaps the most touching story of all is that of the two disciples going to Emmaus; out of His very love for them, He blindfolded them and then made them look for Him, while He put them off the scent by pretending that He knew nothing about all the things that had been happening in Jerusalem; and then when His moment was come "their eyes were opened and they knew Him." (Luke 24: 31). He treats His children in the same way still, He constantly hides Himself from them, leaves them alone to fight and struggle in desolation, solitude and spiritual darkness, and then sometimes shows by His sudden presence how near He has been all the time.

Let me consider two questions:

1. *How does He hide Himself?* (1) Behind obstacles that He makes: suffering, desolation, darkness, temptation, scruples, failure (spiritual as well as temporal), uncongenial people and surroundings—all those many forms of the cross which the true disciple knows so well. Let us remember that *He* is hidden in them, it will make all the difference. (2) Behind obstacles that we ourselves make. This is not so consoling. He has every right to hide Himself from me, but I have no right to make His coming to me difficult by obstacles that I put in His path, and yet how often I do it! Self is the great obstacle. I am taken up with myself, with my own shortcomings and miseries and failures and weaknesses, with my imagination (how it runs away with me, away from Him!) and my fears, my introspection—uselessly looking into myself to see how I am advancing. What are all these but obstacles which keep God at a distance? The soul that attracts Him is the soul that is occupied with Him, not with self.

2. *Why does He hide Himself?* Why does He deliberately set up obstacles which prevent the soul from seeing Him? Why does a mother hide from her child? Is it not for the joy of seeing it look for her and for the consolation she is going to give it in letting herself be found? It is the same with our God Who hides Himself. He wants to make us look for Him, He wants to increase our love, our desire and our merit, He wants

to make us strong in faith and confidence, while acknowledging our helplessness and dependence and nothingness without Him.

Point II.

"Your Life Is Hid With Christ in God."

Though Jesus was hidden in Mary, He was never hidden from her. This was (1) because Mary never put any obstacle between herself and Jesus—her thoughts were all with Him and never with herself, and (2) because her faith and love and desire were so strong that she at once overcame all obstacles, which He in His love and desire for her merit put in her way as was the case during the three days' loss. Jesus and Mary are the models of my interior life. Like Mary I must try to surmount all obstacles, welcome every sword that pierces, leave self and seek Him. Like Jesus in Mary I must strive to lead a hidden life.

How is it to be done? There is only one way—to have God always before my eyes, and self only there to be sacrificed. If I make this my rule, it will simplify my life and be the quick solution of many problems. Why this *dryness* in prayer? To bring God to my mind and to give me an opportunity of sacrificing self with its love of spiritual consolation and sensible enjoyment. The very dryness makes me thirst after God: "As the hart panteth after the fountains of water, so my soul panteth after Thee, O God. My soul hath thirsted after the strong living God; when shall I come and appear before the face of God?" (Ps. 41: 1-3). This is what God wants—to see the soul longing and thirsting for Him. That is why He puts the obstacle of dryness between Himself and the soul, and hides Himself behind it while He watches the soul struggling to forget itself and saying: "O my soul why dost thou disquiet me? Hope thou in God, for I will still give praise to Him" (verse 12). This is how the faithful soul overcomes the obstacles—not by praying to have them removed, but by a firm faith that God is in them. So with temptations—why these terrible temptations, when God could so easily remove them? Because He is the Master and He knows what is best. If the temptations were removed, the soul would soon be wrapped up in self-complacency and self-satisfaction. Temptations properly used keep the soul close to God, it sees God hidden in them and forgetting all about its treacherous self, it turns to Him Who alone can save it from falling, it keeps God only in view and makes the sacrifice of self. The same principle holds good for all the many obstacles behind which God hides. If they are properly used they are no longer obstacles, but stepping-stones by means of which we pass to Him. God everywhere and self nowhere! God everything and self nothing! God, not self, the object of all I do and think and plan! And that not because I can feel Him and see Him and enjoy Him, but because my faith tells me that though hidden *He is there*. This was the principle of Mary's life hidden with her Son. He was the cause, the direct cause, of all her troubles, of all the many swords that pierced her most pure heart, yet never was there a life hidden with Christ as was Mary's and the reason was that she forgot herself and saw JESUS only.

"*Your* life is hid with Christ in God." Are these words of St. Paul true about me? Let me read the whole verse and then I shall know: "For *you are dead*, and your life is hid with Christ in God." *When* self is dead, then I shall be able to say *God only*, and till then, God be thanked, I can hide my miserable self in Him and tell Him that I want it to be sacrificed though I so seldom have the courage to do it.

Colloquy with JESUS hidden in Mary.

Resolution. To see my hidden God everywhere and self nowhere.

Spiritual Bouquet. "Why hidest Thou Thy Face?" (Job 13: 24).

— ❧ —

The Interior Life. (5) Prayer.

"Behold I come that I should do Thy Will: O my God, I have desired it, and Thy law in the midst of my heart." (Ps. 39: 8, 9).

1st. Prelude. Vas spirituale. Vas insigne devotionis.
2nd. Prelude. Grace to "pray without ceasing." (1 Thess. 5: 17).

POINT I.
THE SPIRIT OF PRAYER.

Amongst all the lessons that JESUS living in Mary teaches us, that on prayer must ever hold a foremost place. What is Prayer? "The lifting up of the heart and mind to God," the Catechism tells us. To love God, then, and to think about Him is to pray. JESUS lived in Mary uniquely to do the Will of His Father. He and the Father were *one*—one heart, one mind. He took pleasure in all that concerned His Father: "Hallowed be Thy Name, Thy Kingdom come, Thy Will be done on earth as it is in Heaven." He taught us to pray in the same way, taking our thoughts away from ourselves to our Father, and when we do ask for something for ourselves, letting it be just a short prayer for mercy or for help, acknowledging our weakness and misery and nothingness, while we keep our eyes fixed on our Father—He God, I His creature; He everything, I nothing. "God be merciful to me a sinner," this prayer contains all we need.

O my little Jesus, Who didst think of me in Thy communion with Thy Father, for Thou didst come to do His Will, and His Will was that I should be saved, teach me to think of Thee and to love Thee so much that my life, too, may be one perpetual prayer, that is, that communion with God may be the attitude of my soul.

Point II.

Mary's Spirit of Prayer.

She was ever holding colloquies with her God within her, pondering things over in her heart, that is, talking them over with Him from Whom she had no secrets and between Whom and her soul she put no obstacles. Her life was spent with Him; whatever her duties might be, everything was done with Him, that is prayer. If duties or conservation demanded all her attention for a while, did it matter? No, for He was there all the same. He, in her, carried on the blessed converse with His Father; there was never any separation between Mary and the Blessed Fruit of her womb, Jesus. She would come back to Him with all the more joy, and tell Him what she had been doing and saying. Oh, blessed life of union between Jesus and Mary! Teach me, my Mother, what prayer is. Thou didst understand it so well. It was prayer that made thy life interior for thou wast ever communing with Him Who was *within* thee. "O Mother of the Word, despise not my words."

Point III.

"Learn of Me."

When we think of Jesus praying for nine months to His Father, when we think of Mary's nine months' colloquy with Jesus, we begin to think that there is something wrong about our methods of prayer, that they need re-modelling. Let us try to understand something of what His prayer was. We think of Him, and quite rightly, as talking over with His Father all His plans for man's salvation, praying for each individual thing that would be connected with it through all time. We love to think that He prayed particularly for each one of us. But all this was not the *essence* of His prayer, if it were, we might well be discouraged and feel that we could never copy such a model; our distractions and fatigues, our ignorance and want of memory, to say nothing of our times of dryness and distaste for prayer would make such prayers, except perhaps now and again in times of consolation, impossible for us. Am I to turn away sadly then from Mary this time, saying: It is too hard for me, I cannot copy thy Son here? No, rather let me ask what was the essence of His prayer? What was it which lay behind all? It was the *intention*. And what was that? We have meditated upon it many times: "*Behold I come to do Thy Will, O my God.*" The essence of His prayer was: Thy Will be done and I am here to do it. Naturally there are many different ways of doing that Will, and many degrees in the perfection with which it is done; and that is why we are quite safe in picturing to ourselves Jesus in the womb of His Mother forgetting no single detail; or perhaps a truer picture would be a union with His Father so perfect that everything lay open before them both, and that there was no need to talk about what was so evident. Now let me apply all this to myself and I shall find that instead of being discouraging it is most encouraging, instead of making my prayers harder it will make them far easier. What is my intention in my prayers? Is it not to please God and to do His Will? What does my Morning Offering mean, but that the prayers, work and sufferings of the day are all offered to Him? I form then my *intention* for the day, and as long as I do not deliberately take back that intention, it is there, even if I forget to renew it each morning. Now let me see how this works out in practice. I pay a Visit to our Lord, perhaps I am too tired to think about Him, I may even sleep in His presence; perhaps I am so busy that I find it impossible to keep away distracting thoughts; perhaps I am more taken up with the spiritual book I am reading than with Him—the time is up and I go, thinking, perhaps, what is the good of paying Him a Visit like that? There is great good even in that Visit which all the same might have been so much more perfect. What was my intention in paying it? Certainly to please Him. Then I *have* pleased Him. It was a pleasure to Him to see me come in and sit with Him, even though I was occupied with my own concerns most of the time. We are too much taken up with asking *how* we say our prayers, but the important question is *why* do we say them. To go and sit in His presence, because He is lonely or because I am tired and I would rather sit with Him than with anyone else is *prayer*, even if I say nothing. What God is doing for me is of far more importance to my soul than what I am doing for God; and all the time that I am there, whether I am thinking of Him or not, He is impressing His image on my soul, and this is true, if I am in the state of grace, not only of my stated times of prayer, but of all the day long and the night too. What God wants in our prayers is simplicity. To help us to understand what simplicity is, let us think of a little child with its mother. The mother gives it something to play with or something to do. Is she very much concerned about *what* the child is doing or *how* it is doing it? Not at all, that is of no consequence; nothing it does can be of any real *service* to the mother; but there is something that concerns her very much, and that is whether her child loves her, is happy to be with her, and wants to please her. We are only children and God is more tender than the tenderest mother. It makes very little difference to Him what we are doing while we are with Him or even how we do it (how can our little services make any difference to Him!); but whether or no we love Him, whether or no we care to be with Him, whether or no we want to please Him, these things make all the difference.

Colloquy with JESUS and Mary about prayer.

Resolution. To try to live more in the spirit of prayer.

Spiritual Bouquet. "Let nothing hinder thee from praying *always*" (Ecclus. 18: 22).

— ❧ —

The Interior Life. (6)
Zeal.

"Behold I come that I should do Thy Will. O my God, I have desired it, and Thy law in the midst of my heart." (Ps. 39: 8, 9).

1st. Prelude. JESUS living in and working through Mary.
2nd. Prelude. The grace of zeal according to His methods.

There is a very close connection between prayer and zeal; the more perfect the prayer, the greater necessarily will be the zeal. Why? Because prayer is identifying oneself with the mind and Will of God, and doing everything with the unique intention of pleasing Him. What are the Will and pleasure of God? The salvation of the world for which He became incarnate—The closer we unite ourselves to God in prayer, the dearer will His intentions be to us. The best workers are those who pray best, those who enter most deeply into God's Will and plans. When we find our zeal flagging, it would be well to examine ourselves on our spirit of prayer.

POINT I.

THE ZEAL OF JESUS LIVING IN MARY.

This zeal showed itself at once. No sooner had He become incarnate than He inspired His Mother to take a difficult journey into the "hill country" to visit her cousin Elizabeth. The zeal of JESUS showed itself first of all, as it naturally would, on His Mother and filled her spirit with the humility and charity and forgetfulness of self which were needed for the journey. It then effected Elizabeth and filled her with the Holy Ghost, but these were only the overflowings of His zeal on His way to make what Father Faber calls His "first convert." The soul of John the Baptist, His chosen Precursor, was very precious to Him and as yet it lay unconscious at a distance from God in darkness and the shadow of death. One of the first acts of God Incarnate was to deliver that soul from prison and let it see what great things He had in store for it. At the sound of the voice of the Mother with her Child, a change was wrought in that dark soul; it was set free from the curse of original sin, it was flooded with grace, it was brought nigh to God, the Holy Ghost with all His gifts took possession of it and as a consequence, it leapt in the womb in joy and gratitude and adoration.

The voice of Mary directed by her Child had simultaneously worked two miracles of grace. Elizabeth heard the salutation first, but it was the leaping of the Babe in her womb which made her understand that the Incarnation had taken place, and cry with a loud voice: "Blessed art thou among women and blessed is the Fruit of thy womb."

If the zeal of JESUS was so powerful during the first hours of His life, what must it not have effected during the nine months! How many souls without knowing (as St. John the

Baptist did) the cause, were brought nearer to Heaven by the presence of the Incarnate God in the world!

POINT II.

MARY'S ZEAL.

We have no need to dwell at any length on the zeal of her whom JESUS used as His instrument during the nine months. Mary's was a zeal which compelled her to spend and be spent in the service of those whom JESUS loved; and the secret of its force was the interior life which she lived with her Son—a perfect union of will and purpose with His.

Let me try to copy my Mother in her interior life and then I may hope that her Son will use me too as an instrument of some of His zeal for souls. He must use someone, for He has made Himself as dependent now in the Tabernacle as He was during the time that He lived in Mary. He has deliberately put Himself in the position of *needing* instruments for His work and He will naturally choose those who are most imbued with His spirit and who are willing to adopt His methods. Such an instrument was Mary. She put no obstacles in His way, because she had no will apart from His, her zeal was only a reflexion of His.

POINT III.

"LEARN OF ME."

If I am to fashion my zeal after the pattern of the zeal of JESUS, I must be careful to see that my methods are the same as His. What were His?

(1) *Solitude.* Such was His solitude that no one but Mary knew that He was there. He chose solitude not only during this first stage but during the greater part of His life on earth, and He chooses it still in His

Eucharistic life. It must then be a very necessary accompaniment to zeal. *"Learn of Me."* What am I to learn? That if my zeal is to be efficacious I must live a hermit's life far from the haunts of men? Not necessarily. It would be possible to do this without finding the solitude that begets zeal; and it is quite possible to find the necessary solitude even in the midst of the world's tumult. To say that I have no opportunities for doing good because I am in uncongenial surroundings, or because I am obliged by my circumstances to lead a lonely life or to live where there is apparently no scope for work for souls is to fail to understand what zeal is. Why do people shut themselves up in convents, cries the world, when they might do so much good outside? Uniquely because of their zeal for souls—they have sufficient courage to adopt Our Lord's methods. If I am one whom He has trusted with the trial of loneliness in my life, let me cultivate a devotion to Him in His Mother's womb, and let me take heart and be of good courage. All the activity in the world that is of any use is of use because of the prayer that is behind it. *Whose* prayers who shall say? They may be *mine* if I live an interior life, for those who live in the retreat of their own heart with God have a limitless scope for their zeal.

(2) *Silence.* Zeal for God and His work does not depend then, on words. I need not be troubled because I am not eloquent, or because I have an impediment in my speech, or because I never know what to say. How could such things matter to God, the Omnipotent God! He could alter them in a moment if necessary. The Word Himself Who could have spoken so attractively and with such power was silent for most of His

life. The time He chose for His Incarnation was "while all things were in quiet silence and the night was in the midst of her course" (Wisdom 18: 14); and He is silent still in the Tabernacle; He loves silence, and the more the soul is interior, the more it will adopt His method of silence and the more it will understand what a marvellous help it is to zeal. How can this be? Because the silence that we choose to keep for God means shutting out all else, that we may talk to Him alone. Could there be a better method than this for making us zealous for the work so dear to His Heart?

(3) *Obedience.* Think of His obedience in the womb of His Mother. His very Incarnation was an act of obedience, He waited for Mary's *Fiat.* His waiting for nine months was purely an act of obedience to the laws of nature, for His Soul and Body were perfect from the moment of His conception. All the time that He lived in Mary, He obeyed all whom she obeyed— St. Joseph, the Roman Emperor, the people at Bethlehem. He gave up His own Will to others.

This was His method of being zealous. This is how He did the work that He had come to do. Can I adopt this method? It is not easy. I do so love to follow my own sweet will especially when I am working for the souls of others. I feel that no one has a right to dictate to me, that my work ought to be spontaneous, not cramped nor confined nor limited nor any other adjective that the devil can persuade me to use, if only he can make me believe that it is a blessed thing to be independent! If my zeal for God is to be worth anything, let me follow the methods of God Incarnate in the womb of His Mother and be absolutely obedient to God, to His Holy Church and to those whom I ought to obey.

(4) *Poverty.* "You know the grace of our Lord JESUS Christ, that being rich, He became poor for your sakes, that through His poverty you might be rich" (2 Cor. 8: 9). In His zeal for our wealth, He made Himself poor, He deliberately adopted poverty as one of His methods in His life of zeal. Poverty is the voluntary laying aside of all that we might have, in order that our purpose may be single. All can do this whether rich or poor, for all have much that they would rather not lay on one side, and *all* have *self.* Let us think what the Eternal Word was as God, and then what He was in Mary's womb, and we shall understand what poverty means. If we are to be zealous in His service, we must not only understand, but copy.

(5) *Patience.* Patience is a twofold grace, that of *waiting* and that of *suffering*, both are a great aid to zeal. The Eternal Word's zeal for the salvation of men had existed in all its perfection and all its fulness from all eternity, yet think how long He waited! When the conditions were changed and He had at length become incarnate, He still waited patiently for nine months, and after that He waited for thirty years! This was zeal, zeal in its *perfection.* Is my zeal tempered with patience? Am I patient with souls, patient with myself, patient above all when God says: *Wait*, do nothing?

JESUS showed His patience in the womb of His Mother not only by waiting; but by suffering, as we have already seen, all the inconveniences that were incident to His new existence. He doubtless also forestalled all the sufferings that were in store for Him and offered them all to His Father. Zeal without the aid of suffering cannot go far and it was one of the methods He chose. If I have not courage enough to *choose* it, I must, if my zeal is to be at all like His, be ready for it when He chooses it for me.

It will probably be seen one day that those whose lives have been lives of suffering, and who have never been able to do any active work for Him, are those whose zeal has effected the most for His glory and His Kingdom.

Those of us who are not entrusted with this wonderfully blessed gift of suffering, can at any rate offer to Him for souls all the many little inconveniences and incommodities of our lives, and so copy to some small extent the life of JESUS hidden in Mary.

O my little JESUS, help me, at whatever cost to self, to copy Thee.

> *Colloquy* with JESUS hidden in Mary, asking Him for grace, so to adopt His methods that He may use me as an instrument of His zeal.
>
> *Resolution.* Not to shrink from adopting His methods.
>
> *Spiritual Bouquet.* "Every one that hath zeal ... let him follow Me" (1 Macc. 2: 27).

— ❧ —

O Sapientia!

December 17th.

"O Wisdom Who camest forth from the mouth of the Most High, reaching from end to end mightily, and disposing all things sweetly, come and teach us the way of prudence!" (Vide Wisdom 8: 1*).*

1st. Prelude. The Tabernacle of the hidden God.
2nd. Prelude. The grace of prudence.

For seven days before the Vigil of Christmas, the Church makes use of seven solemn antiphons, commonly known as the "Seven O's," because they all begin with "O." One is sung every day at Vespers reminding us that Our Lord is to come in the evening of the world's history. They are a sort of cry or invitation of the Church, address-ing her Bridegroom by some spiritual title and begging Him to come. Before and after the *Magnificat* is the time the Church chooses for these solemn antiphons in order to keep constantly before our minds the truth that He is coming by Mary. As the days of Advent draw nearer to their close, this truth is plainly marked in the Mass. The Epistle, Gospel and Communion for Ember Wednesday (in the third week) are all full of Mary; the Gospel for Ember Friday gives the account of the Visitation; the Mass for the Fourth Sunday of Advent, as if the Church were loath to leave her out, brings Mary in at the Offertory and Communion; and that for the Vigil of Christmas devotes its Gospel to her. Let us then as we meditate on these great antiphons look in the direction of Mary where our King is as yet hidden, remembering that it is she who when Christmas comes, is going to shew unto us the Blessed Fruit of her womb JESUS.

Point I.

"O Wisdom That Proceedest From the Mouth of the Most High."

He is the *Eternal* Wisdom, and He has now become the *Incarnate* Wisdom. It is to Him that the Church is calling today. He is the "Wisdom of God" (1 Cor. 1: 24) and the Source of all wisdom; and yet as man the Spirit of God has rested upon Him and filled His human Soul with the seven-fold gifts, of which Wisdom is the first. This gift enabled Him as man to know all mysteries, all God's secret designs and plans, and to enjoy to the full all His perfections. The subject is so vast that it seems impossible for me to meditate about it, but I will take one of the many things which the Holy Scriptures say about Wisdom, one which will lead me again to the Sanctuary where I would be.

"God loveth none but him that dwelleth with Wisdom" (Wisdom 7: 28). He so loved His poor fallen world that He gave His only begotten Son to be incarnate for it, and now all He asks from His children in return is their love and that they should show it by dwelling with Him. He came to be *Emmanuel*, God with us. He tabernacled among us, and what His Father asks is that we should not shun Him and live far away from Him, but that we should dwell with Him. Let me keep close then in spirit to His blessed Mother, the Tabernacle where my God is hidden, and let me keep close in reality to the Tabernacle on the Altar where He is expecting my confidences as surely as He expected those of His Mother; let me treat Him as my Friend to Whom I can tell everything that concerns me—how anxious I am to desire Him to come and yet how little desire I seem to have. There is a way of dwelling with Him which is even closer still: "He that eateth My Flesh and drinketh My Blood abideth in Me and I in him" (John 6: 57).

This is the extension of the Incarnation, the way that Infinite Wisdom devised by which poor fallen man could nevertheless dwell with Wisdom.

O Eternal Wisdom, help me to make better use of this Thy most wonderful plan for continuing the Incarnation! He was incarnate for me in the womb of the Blessed Virgin, but He is incarnate for me in a more special and personal way each time that I receive Him in Holy Communion. By means of my Communions and their effects I can dwell always without any interruption in the tabernacle of the Most High, for it is of me that Eternal Wisdom speaks when He says: "My Father will love him, and We will come to him and will make Our abode with him." (John 14: 23).

POINT II.

"REACHING FROM END TO END MIGHTILY AND DISPOSING ALL THINGS SWEETLY."

Wisdom "can do all things" (Wisdom 7: 27) and it is God hidden in the womb of Mary, Who is reaching from end to end of the earth and ordering the whole world to be enrolled everyone in his own city. Why was this? Because the Roman Emperor wanted to know the number of the subjects in his vast empire just to satisfy his ambition? This is the answer the world would give, but in this case the children of Light—the children of the Incarnate Wisdom know better. The world is being agitated, though it does not know it, not by the command of any earthly monarch, but by the King of kings Who is about to be born and Who must fulfil a certain prophecy as to His birthplace. The prophet Micaias said of Him: "His going forth is from the beginning, from the days of eternity. And thou, Bethlehem Ephrata art a little one among the thousands of Juda; *out of thee shall He come*" (chap. 5: 2); and Mary, the mother who had been destined from all eternity to give birth to Him Who was "from the days of eternity," was living quietly at *Nazareth* making all her preparations for His birth there. But could not God have devised means to send Mary to Bethlehem without disturbing the whole world? Yes, but He would show to those who have eyes to see, that wisdom "*can* do all things," that though He is to all appearances helpless, hidden and dependent, yet it is He and not any other Who is King of the whole world, and that even now before His birth He can reach from end to end of it mightily and do what He will therein. And so "there went out a decree from Caesar Augustus that the whole world should be enrolled ... everyone in his own city," and Joseph and Mary went to Bethlehem and it so happened (as we should say) "that when they were there, her days were accomplished, that she should be delivered" (Luke 2: 1-6) and the King was born in *Bethlehem*. Sweetly He had ordered all things to suit His divine purpose.

POINT III.

"COME AND TEACH US THE WAY OF PRUDENCE."

Come, my little King, Who art nevertheless the Eternal Wisdom, come and teach me this heavenly prudence. I know Thy power and I know Thy gentleness. I know, that is to say, that Thou *canst* do everything and that Thou art disposing sweetly everything in my life; but I want Thee to come and teach me to put my knowledge into practice. If the whole world could be set in motion by Thee just in order that one little desire of Thy Divine Providence might be fulfilled, shall I not be ready to own that Thou art indeed the King, that whatever may happen in the earth, it is the Lord Who *reigneth*; and in my own life when things seem, as they sometimes do, inexplicable and beyond all human ken, Oh! come and teach me that the way of prudence is to lie still like a little child in its mother's arms, not to try to fathom nor to understand, but to say: I am in the Arms of the Eternal Wisdom, Who can do all things, Who loves me with an infinite love and Who is disposing all things sweetly, gently, mercifully for my sake.

This is the lesson the Child yet unborn would teach. His Mother understood, for, as we have seen, one principle guided the two lives; but it was not easy for her to have all her plans disarranged, to hear that she and her husband must take a long journey perhaps of two or three days, to know that her Son could not be born in her own little home so dear to her with all its hallowed memories, to know that she could not lay Him in the little cradle that she had so lovingly prepared for Him nor surround Him with the little comforts that she had been able to provide. All this would have been much even for a rich mother to give up, and Mary was poor and she knew that she and Joseph would have to take just what they could get and no more. Yet in Mary's heart there was no anxiety, no murmuring, no hesitation, no regret even. Why? Because the Babe within her taught her prudence, taught her, that is, that God's ways are best, that it was He Who was ordering all things sweetly, and that if her plans were upset, it simply meant that they did not happen to be God's plans; and she willingly gave up hers for His.

O Mary as I kneel before the Tabernacle where Thy Son as yet lies hidden, present my petitions to Him. Tell Him that, cost what it may, I do want His Will to be done, I do want to realize that it is He Who is ordering all things sweetly for me and that though the way is often difficult it is *His* way and therefore mine—"the way of prudence."

Colloquy with the Incarnate Wisdom.

Resolution. "I purposed therefore to take her (Wisdom) to me to live with me, knowing that she will communicate to me of her good things" (Wisdom 8: 9).

Spiritual Bouquet. "O Sapientia! ... come and teach us the way of prudence."

— ❧ —

O Adonai!

December 18th. Feast of the Expectation of Our Lady.

"O Adonai and Leader of the House of Israel! Who appearedst to Moses in the fire of the flaming bush and gavest him the law on Sinai. Come and redeem us by Thy outstretched arm." (Ex. 6: 3, 3: 1-9, 20: 18-22).

1st. Prelude. The Tabernacle of the Hidden God.
2nd. Prelude. Grace to expect and desire with Mary.

POINT I.
"O VIRGO VIRGINUM!"

We think again today of the Mother as well as of the Son. There is another "O" which is in the Vespers of the Feast of the Expectation together with the "*O Adonai!*" and that is "*O Virgo virginum!*" We appeal again then to Mary asking her to show us how to wait, how to desire, how to love, how to worship. Let us try to think what her feelings must have been during these last few days. She is preparing for her journey, putting together the few necessaries that they could take, packing up the little "swaddling clothes," and all the time thinking of nothing but her Son, Whose Face she is now so soon to see. The joy of the expectation is so great that it overshadows all else—she can talk of and think of nothing but His birth, now so near, and it is to *Him* that she talks. All her secrets, all her longings, all her hopes, all her words of love and joy are for Him. This is the interior life.

As the great day approaches is my interior life becoming more intense? Are all my desires centred on the little One Who is coming? Am I continually holding converse with Him, telling Him all that is in my heart? Is He the centre of all my preparations for Christmas? Is the real Christmas joy, that is, the joy caused by the thought of His Coming, so great that it puts into the shade all difficulties, sorrows, disappointments and inconveniences? Mary's troubles were all caused by JESUS. If it had not been for the prophecy which said He must be born in Bethlehem she would not have had to leave her home at such an inconvenient moment and at such an inclement season of the year.

When shall I learn that all my troubles come directly from JESUS too, and from my union with Him? When I do, I shall have peace, the peace which Mary had and which a really interior life cannot fail to produce. If I find that my peace is easily disturbed by passing events, let me examine my conscience as to my interior life and I shall probably find the reason.

POINT II.

O ADONAI ET DUX!

O Lord and *Leader*! "Give ear, O Thou that rulest Israel, Thou that *leadest* Joseph like a sheep!" ("Introit" for Advent II and "Gradual" for Advent III). This is the idea in the Church's cry today, she is saluting her General. He it is Who though as yet hidden is nevertheless leading all. He it is Who slowly though surely has been leading the world through many phases till it is ready for its Creator to come and live upon it. He it is Who has led Joseph like a sheep—carefully watched over the chosen nation, because He Himself, when the time came, was to be born in it. He it is Who led the prophets, carefully guiding their hands to write of Him and making their prophecies more and more lucid as the day approached. He it is Who is now leading the whole world and placing everybody in his own city. He it is Who is leading Joseph away from Nazareth. He it is Who is leading His own Mother over every step of that difficult and tiring journey, letting the joy in His own Heart overflow into hers; and He is *my* Leader too. With such a General, nothing will be overlooked in my life; everything will be arranged in wisdom and love. I need have no fear, no anxiety on that account; but such a Leader expects a whole-hearted, unswerving allegiance from His followers. He expects not only their obedience, but their loyalty and their love. Does He demand these by force? No, for He is a *Leader*, not a driver. "He calleth His own sheep by name and *leadeth* them.... He goeth before them and the sheep follow Him" (John 10: 3, 4). What are His methods? The Incarnation with all its consequences. He made Himself a *man*, not an angel, because He wanted to attract man to Himself, to win his love. He identified Himself with man, because He wanted man to identify himself with Him. The church, the Holy Eucharist, the Tabernacle, Holy Communion, His Sacred Heart—all these are to attract men to follow Him. He is there in each of these going before and leading men on. He is appealing to them now from the womb of His Mother, suggesting to them that they should choose suffering and humiliation and the hidden life, because He chose them and loved them and submitted to them for us; they were His methods, and His object in becoming incarnate for us was to win our love to such an extent that we should take Him as our Leader and adopt His methods.

Oh! come, little Leader, come and redeem us. I for one am determined to follow wheresoever Thou dost lead, "in what place soever Thou shalt be, my Lord King, either in death or in life there will Thy servant be" (2 Kings 15: 21). "Behold I have given Him for a Leader" (Is. 55: 4).

POINT III.
THE OUTSTRETCHED ARM.

The outstretched arm is a sign (1) of *power*. The little One Whom we are expecting, though so winning and gentle and loving, is nevertheless the Almighty and All-powerful God. He it is Who said: "I made the earth and the men and the beasts that are upon the earth by My great power and by My stretched out arm" (Jer. 27: 5). He it is Who said of those who would not acknowledge Him as their King: "I will Myself fight against you with an outstretched hand and with a strong arm" (chap. 21: 5). He it is Who "with a strong hand and a stretched-out arm" delivered His people of old out of the land of Egypt (Deut. 26: 8). He it is Who gave the law on Sinai, when "the thunders began to be heard and lightning to flash and a very thick cloud to cover the mount, and the noise of the trumpet sounded exceeding loud and the people ... feared." Why? Because "the Lord came down upon Mount Sinai in the very top of the mount" (Ex. 19: 16, 20). He came then in power to give with His own outstretched arm His commandments to His people; but now He is coming in the silence of the night to win them by His love and no one will be afraid of a little Child.

Oh! come, and redeem us by Thy stretched out arm. Come in all Thy might to save us from our sins—our past sins and the evil habits they have left, our present attachment to venial sins which we are ashamed of, but are obliged to confess lingers still; come and deliver us from our countless imperfections: "Lord if Thou wilt, Thou canst make me clean" (Matt. 8: 2).

The outstretched arm is also a sign (2) of *pity*, of *yearning*, of *longing*. A mother stretches out her arms to receive her babe taking its first tottering steps, to welcome her prodigal, to protect those in danger, to help in every time of need.

When God was longing to deliver His people of old from the cruel bondage in Egypt, He attracted Moses' attention by a burning bush, so that He could tell him of His yearnings towards His people. Moses saw that the bush was on fire and was not burnt and he said: "I will go and see why the bush is not burnt" (Ex. 3: 2-3). That bush hid two mysteries which were beyond Moses' power of reason, but God revealed them later to His Saints. The fire that burned was the Divinity and the bush which was impregnated by the fire and yet not burnt was the Sacred Humanity. Again, the bush was a figure of Mary who though she received the God-Man into her sacred womb yet remained a virgin—the bush held the flame of fire which lighted the whole world and yet remained intact. Moses though he did not see the things which we see, nevertheless saw a "great sight" and "when the Lord saw that he went forward to see, He called to him out of the midst of the bush" and told him not to come too near and to take off his shoes for the ground was holy. He then told him Who He was and why He had come: "I have seen the afflictions of My people.... I have heard their cry ... and knowing their sorrow, I am come down to deliver them" (verses 7, 8). It was the Heart of God yearning for His children. His Hands were stretched out in pity and love, but His hour was not yet. He waited and "when the fulness of the time was come, God sent His Son" (Gal. 4: 4); and now we are kneeling before the Sanctuary wherein He has still a few days to wait; we have turned aside to see the "great sight," we know that we are treading on holy ground. "*Rubum quem viderat Moyses incombustum conservatam agnovimus tuam laudabilem virginitatem; Dei genitrix intercede pro nobis.*" In the bush which Moses saw unconsumed, we acknowledge thy admirable virginity preserved: intercede for us, O Mother of God. (Little Office. B. V. M.—A Christmas antiphon).

As we keep near to the Burning Bush we wonder more and more at the mystery; we ask why, but we never receive a satisfying answer, for who can fathom the mystery of the love of God? The Word is silent yet. Could He speak, we should hear the same words as Moses heard, for the Heart of God changes not: "I have seen the afflictions of My people.... I am come down to deliver them." How intense were His yearnings! How great was His expectation! Let me try to make Him some little return by my desires and my yearnings for Him! Oh! come, little Saviour, come and redeem us by Thy outstretched Arm!

Colloquy with Him Who is so soon to come.

Resolution. To wait with His Mother today asking her to give me some of her desire.

Spiritual Bouquet. "A little Child shall lead them" (Is. 11: 6).

— ❧ —

O Radix Jesse!

December 19th.

"*O Root of Jesse! Who standest as the ensign of the people, before Whom Kings shall keep silence and unto Whom the nations shall make their supplication, come and set us free, tarry now no longer.*" (Vide Is. 11: 10 and Apoc. 22: 16).

1st. Prelude. The Tree of Jesse so often seen carved on cathedral porches and painted on windows, and in Missals.

2nd. Prelude. Grace to rally under the Standard of the Tree of Jesse.

Point I.
The Root of Jesse.

"There shall come forth a Rod out of the Root of Jesse, and a Flower shall rise up out of his Root; and the Spirit of the Lord shall rest upon Him: the Spirit of Wisdom and of Understanding, the Spirit of Counsel and of Fortitude, the Spirit of Knowledge and of Godliness; and He shall be filled with the Spirit of the Fear of the Lord" (Is. 11: 1-3). St. Jerome says that the Branch is Our Lady and the Flower her Son, Who says of Himself: "I am the Flower of the field and the Lily of the valleys" (Cant. 2: 1); and a responsory dating from the middle ages says: "R. The Root of Jesse gave out a Branch: and the Branch a Flower; and on the Flower resteth the Holy Spirit. V. The Virgin Mother of God is the Branch, her Son is the Flower, and on the Flower resteth the Holy Spirit."

So once again, if we would find the Flower we must first find the Branch which bears it. The Flower is still in bud but presently it will open, and its beauty and fragrance will fill the whole earth and attract all men to it: "What manner of one is thy Beloved of the beloved, O thou most beautiful among women?" "My Beloved is white and ruddy, chosen out of thousands" (Cant. 5: 9, 10). I can understand that thy beautiful Lily is white, for I know that such is His purity that even the heavens are not pure in His sight, but why is His apparel *red*? (Is. 63: 2). Because He is "clothed with a garment sprinkled with blood: and His name is called: *The Word of God*" (Apoc. 19: 13). Even now, before His delicate petals are unfolded, they are marked with the Cross.

O Root of Jesse, can ever tree compare with thine—one of whose branches was found worthy to bear a Flower so fair! There are further beauties as we gaze—a heavenly Dew is resting on the Flower, it is the Holy Spirit Himself, Who at that blest moment when He overshadowed the Branch poured out all His choicest gifts upon the Flower. As God, the seven-fold gifts were His from all eternity, and directly the Human-ity was united to the Eternal Word, the divine perfections belonged to it, so that as man "He was made unto us the *Wis-dom* of *God*" and could understand all mysteries. By the gift of *Understanding* He knew and entered into all God's plans for the Redemption of the world. The gift of *Counsel* showed Him exactly what was the Will of His Father which He had come to do. The gift of *Fortitude* gave Him the strength to carry out His Father's Will and to say ever: Not My Will but Thine be done. His *Knowledge* was so profound that He pre-ferred poverty to riches, and to be despised rather than to be honoured; He knew as Man the true worth of the thing which as God He had created. The gift of *Piety* established that tender relationship between Him and His Father which He wished us to have when He taught us to say: *Our Father*; it included also His perfect relationship with His Mother and St. Joseph. The gift of *Fear* gave Him as Man a reverence and respect for the majesty of God. (*Vide* Heb. 5: 7).

It was thus that the heavenly Dew rested on the heavenly Flower.

O my JESUS, come and tarry no longer! I know that Thou hadst no need of any of these gifts; they rested on Thee because Thou art my Model and Thou wouldst show me how to use them.

POINT II.

THE ENSIGN OF THE PEOPLE.

It is the Tree of Jesse which stands as an ensign, about which Our Lord says: "I am the Root and Stock of David" (Apoc. 22: 16). He then is the Standard-bearer and the

Standard is His Cross. "Bearing His own Cross He went forth" (John 19: 17). He is the "*sign* which shall be contradicted" by His enemies (Luke 2: 34), but when the sign of the Son of Man shall appear in the Heavens (Matt. 24: 30) it will bring joy and hope to the hearts of all those who love His Coming (2 Tim. 4: 8). "My beloved is white and ruddy, chosen out of thousands," or according to another translation: "My beloved is white and ruddy a *Standard bearer*" (Cant. 5: 10 A. V. Margin), chosen for His strength as well as for His beauty. To Him shall the nations make supplication, for He said: "I, if I be lifted up from the earth will draw all things to Myself" (John 12: 32).

There are only two standards in the world—that of JESUS Christ and that of the devil. Both leaders want me to enlist; both are trying to win me; but by what different means! The devil strives to entrap me with the silken threads of sin which seem so insignificant and harmless, but which if I allow myself to be trapped by them, he will twine into a thick rope and hold me fast; while JESUS draws me to Himself with the cords of love. Both are infinitely more powerful than I am, and yet all depends on *me*, that is, on my will. The cords of love are far stronger than the cords of hate, so I need not be afraid of the devil's capturing me against my will; but on the other hand JESUS will not draw me with the cords of love against my will. "*If thou wilt*, ... come," is His method. There *are* chains, there *is* a cross, but all is love. A little Child holds the Standard, a little Child leads, and all He asks is that we should follow Him and do as He does.

Come, then, little JESUS, set up Thy Royal Standard, come, tarry no longer. I am longing to show Thee that I am not going to be a soldier in name only; longing to show Thee that I understand that a soldier who has pledged himself to fight under Thy Standard must adopt Thy methods, that if I would be a soldier on whom Thou canst count, I must be really mortified, really poor, really ready to give up my own will and my own methods, really anxious to have humiliations because I know that there is no other way of attaining the beautiful virtue of humility. I am longing to show Thee that I understand that those who march under Thy Standard must be marked by the Cross. Oh! come, and set me free from all that keeps me from offering myself whole-heartedly for Thy service. Come and cut all the many little cords that still bind me to the service of self. Thy Mother wants Thee, the Angels are longing to look upon Thy Face, the world wants Thee though it knows it not, and I am longing to want Thee too. Oh! teach me to want Thee more.

Colloquy with the Branch and the Flower.

Resolution. To examine myself today as to my attachments.

Spiritual Bouquet. "Come and set us free, tarry now no longer."

— ❧ —

O Clavis David!

December 20th.

"O Key of David and Sceptre of the House of Israel! Who openest and no man shutteth; Who shuttest and no man openeth; come and bring forth from his prison-house the captive sitting in darkness and in the shadow of death." (Isaias 22: 22, Apoc. 3: 7, Gen. 49: 10, Heb. 1: 8).

1st. Prelude. The little King with the Key and the Sceptre.
2nd. Prelude. Grace to respond to the Key and the Sceptre.

Point I.

THE KEY OF DAVID.

"I will lay the Key of the House of David upon His shoulder" (Is. 22: 22). "To the Angel of the Church of Philadelphia write: These things saith the Holy One and the True One, He that hath the Key of David, He that openeth and no man shutteth, shutteth and no man openeth: I know thy works. Behold I have given before thee a door opened which no man can shut, because thou hast a little strength." (Apoc. 3: 7-8).

The Babe unborn has already had the Key laid upon His Shoulder. He already has authority. Soon, very soon now, He will come to use it. How will He use this Key and what is it? It is the Key of authority but it is also the Key of love. (1) He is coming to unlock the gates which hold the human race fast in ignorance and sin, to be its Redeemer, to give it "a door opened which no man can shut," to give it a chance if it will of walking out of its prison-house into the liberty wherewith Christ alone can make it free (Gal. 4: 31). (2) He is coming to put His golden Key of love into the hearts of men, to open those doors which are shut against Him and which none but He can open, for none but He can give grace. Each little child whose heart is filled with grace at its Baptism is only able to receive it because the little Child with the golden Key has opened its heart. "Thou hast opened the Kingdom of Heaven to all believers." Come, then, O Key of David, come and begin Thy blessed work on earth. Thou hast already put Thy magic Key into the heart of St. John the Baptist and doubtless of many another; come and tarry not, come and found Thy Church and pass on the wondrous power of the keys to those with whom Thou wilt leave Thy authority. (3) He is coming to open with His Key of love His own most Sacred Heart. None but He can open that vast treasure-house of love, and none but He can shut it. It will be there for a refuge for all His children in all time—a standing memorial of His love. What does He ask in return? Only that when we hear Him put His golden Key into our hearts, there may be a response: "My Beloved put His Hand through the key-hole and my heart was moved at His touch. I arose up to open to my Beloved" (Cant. 5: 4-5). The rising up to let Him in is our part, He puts in His Key and unlocks, that is, He removes all obstacles by His grace, but we must respond to that grace for though He has unlocked the door He will not force an entrance. "Behold I stand at the door and knock," and then He waits, waits for our correspondence and for our love. "My son, give Me thy heart," He wants it, He has used His Key of love to obtain it, but He will not take it, it must be a free gift of love.

At the last great Advent the door of His mercy will be shut against all those who have refused Him an entrance into their hearts, and when He shuts, no man can open. "Lord, Lord, open to us," and the answer will come through the eternally locked door: "I never knew you, depart from Me."

Oh! come, Divine little One, come with Thy Key while yet there is time and unlock the many hearts which still find no place for Thee, no time to attend to Thee waiting so patiently, no desire to give Thee an invitation this Christmas; and give them grace to respond.

POINT II.

THE SCEPTRE OF THE HOUSE OF ISRAEL.

The little One Who is to come not only has a Key on His Shoulder, but a Sceptre in His Hand. The word used for Sceptre (*shebet*) in the Hebrew has four distinct meanings and we can apply them all to our Lord and Saviour, JESUS Christ. It is:

(1) a rod of *command*, a sign of *royalty* (Esther 4: 11, Ps. 44: 7);
(2) a rod of iron, a rod of *correction* (Ps. 2: 9, Prov. 22: 15);
(3) the *shepherd's* rod or wand (Lev. 27: 32);
(4) the *flail* which separates the grain from the chaff (Is. 28: 27).

(1) *A sign of royalty.* He is my King—how much that says to me! He has authority over me and a right to command me, a right to my service from every Point of view; but He will not exact it from me. He stretches out His Sceptre of mercy in token of clemency. He wants my service, but He wants it to be the outcome of my love and so He uses His Sceptre to attract me. He brings Himself down to my level, He calls Himself my Brother, my Friend. He tells me that if I will throw in my lot with Him and do as He does, one day I shall share His Kingdom and reign with Him. Such is my King and such is the meaning of His Sceptre. "Where is He that is born King of the Jews?" Thou art as yet hidden, O my little King, but Thou wilt be *born* a king for "Thy throne, O God, is for ever and ever, a sceptre of justice is the sceptre of Thy Kingdom" (Heb. 1: 8). What is my response going to be to that Sceptre stretched out once again? That of a loyal, whole-hearted, loving subject or that of one who is still hesitating between the service of self and the service of the King?

(2) *A rod of correction.* For His enemies it is a "rod of iron," but for His children a rod of love, for what son is there whom the father doth not correct? "Whom the Lord loveth He chastiseth; and He scourgeth every son whom He receiveth. Persevere under discipline. God dealeth with you as with His sons." (Heb. 12: 6-7). We

are not to "faint" nor "be weary" nor "neglect the discipline," not to be inclined to give all up and choose an easier path; no, but to regard the discipline as a "consolation," (verse 5) a proof of love, a sign that we are really the children with whom He does what He likes, instructing us according to His own pleasure (verse 10). Oh! my little King, come with Thy rod of correction, come and make me a saint and do not spare me in the making. He that spareth the rod spoileth the child. I do not want to be a spoilt child, but a child on whom Thou canst count, that is, a child to whom Thou canst say what Thou wilt and whom Thou canst criticize as thou wilt, by the mouth of whom Thou wilt, a child whom Thou dost not *consider* because Thou art sure of its love, sure, that is, that it loves Thee and Thy ways better than self and its ways.

(3) *A shepherd's staff or crook.* As it had been prophesied of Him that He should be a king, so it had also been prophesied that He should be a shepherd: "I will save My flock ... and I will set up one Shepherd over them and He shall feed them and He shall be their Shepherd" (Ezech. 34: 22, 23, and 37: 24). "He shall feed His flock like a shepherd, He shall gather together the lambs with His arms, and shall take them up in His bosom, and He Himself shall carry them that are with young" (Is. 40: 11). "I am the Good Shepherd;" even now while He is yet in the womb of His Mother He is counting His sheep, calling them out, knowing each one by name, thinking of the great fold which He is going to make, of the one shepherd to whom He will entrust the great work of feeding His sheep, of the "other sheep" whom He "must bring" into the fold sooner or later. Even now He is planning to lay

down His life for His sheep "that they may have life and have it more abundantly."

(4) *The flail* which separates the chaff from the good grain, the *tribulum* which causes "great *tribulation*" on earth's threshing floor, but which is used only for the good of the grain and ensures its being gathered into the heavenly garners. Oh! my little King, Who art coming to bring peace make me understand that I shall never have peace till I am fully persuaded that all my *tribulation*, all my troubles, trials and afflictions are directly caused by Thee, that it is Thou Thyself and no other Who dost use the threshing instruments to separate me from all that is not pleasing to Thee.

Come then, and with Thy Key of love unlock the prison-house and bring forth the captive sitting in darkness and then with Thy Sceptre rule him, correct him, guide him and afflict him.

Colloquy with Him Who has the Key and the Sceptre.
Resolution. To rise up and open to my Beloved.
Spiritual Bouquet. O Clavis David!

— ❧ —

O Oriens!

December 21st. Feast of St. Thomas.

"O Orient! (Dawn of the East, Rising Sun. Dayspring) Splendour of the Light Eternal and Sun of Justice, come and enlighten them that sit in darkness and in the shadow of death." (Is. 9: 2, Zach. 3: 8, 6: 12, Mal. 4: 2, Luke 1: 78).

1st. Prelude. "The light of the morning when the sun riseth" (2 Kings 23: 4).
2nd. Prelude. Grace to tread always the "Way of Peace."

POINT I.
THE ORIENT.

"Behold I will bring my Servant the Orient." (Zach. 3: 8). Now God has kept His promise for Zachary has already sung: "The Orient from on high has visited us." But where is He, this Servant of God Who has come to do His Will, this Man Who is also God, this Splendour of the Light Eternal and Sun of Justice? As yet He is hiding His light, but "fear not for on the fifth day Our Lord will come unto you" (Antiphon of the *Benedictus* for today). He will come and He will not tarry; but when He comes He will still hide His light under the swaddling clothes and the helplessness and dependence of a little babe. Why is this, O Orient? Thou art the Light Eternal and the Sun of Justice and yet Thy rising seems to make so little difference in the world. Hardly any know that Thou hast risen. My child, it is true that I am the Light of the world, true that I am the bright and morning Star, but the light can only reach the world by faith. Those who have faith like Zachary and his wife and infant son know that I have visited them, not because they have *seen* me, but by faith. It is the same with my own sweet Mother: "Blessed art thou that hast *believed*" (Luke 1: 45). It will be the same when I am born in a few days' time. Most will see nothing beyond a babe in swaddling clothes, but to a chosen few who have the gift of faith the Sun of Justice will have risen, the Star will have appeared, their cry will be: "Behold a Man," even the Man-God, "the Orient is His name." It will be the same all through My life on earth, only the few will recognize the Light of the world; most will not come to Me, but will prefer darkness rather than light. It will be the same with My sacramental life in the Church. I shall be there, but only the eye of faith will detect Me. The Sun of Justice has risen with health in His

Wings, but only very gradually will He make Himself felt in a world that is sitting in darkness and in the shadow of death.

And why, O Orient, Splendour of the Light Eternal, why dost Thou not cast Thy bright beams over the whole world at once that all may know and recognize Thee as the Dayspring which has risen?

Because, My child, I love faith and it is by faith that I intend men to know Me. I do enlighten "every man that cometh into this world" (John 1: 9), that is I give to each sufficient light to save his soul, to one more, to another less, and I shall judge according to the light I have given; but what I want from all is co-operation, I want their faith, I want them to believe, not because they can see and understand, but because by means of My grace in their hearts and especially by means of the revelation given to My Church I enlighten their minds. Yes, the Sun has risen with health in His Wings, and gradually He will increase in strength till the "uttermost parts of the earth" respond to His light. It is a work of time just as it is a work of time in each individual soul. The soul does not see clearly as soon as the light enters; there is a period when men seem like trees walking (Mark 8: 24); but if only it will respond and hold on by faith, the time will come when it will see all things clearly.

O Orient, come and enlighten those that sit in darkness and in the shadow of death with the light of faith. It is faith that is needed on the earth, it is faith that is needed in each individual soul. It is faith that I need, more faith, more con-fidence in Thy dealings. Many shadows are still cast on my soul by sin—even a wilful imperfection casts a shadow. Oh What need I have of Thee, O Orient from on high, to come and visit me and chase away the shadows of the night! "Till the day break and the shadows retire" (Cant. 2: 17, 4: 6).

POINT II.
ST. THOMAS.

It is a coincidence, if not something more, that puts the antiphon *O Oriens!* on the same day as the Feast of St. Thomas. It was on account of St. Thomas' *doubt* that the great principle was given to the Church: "Blessed are they that have not seen and yet have believed." It is on account of St. Thomas' *faith* that countless Indulgences are granted every day to the faithful who make use of his words: "My Lord and my God" when their sight shows them nothing but a little Host elevated by a priest. It was St. Thomas' *zeal* which made him go to the Indies and proclaim that the Orient had visited His people and that God had become incarnate for men. "Thou didst make all the Indies shine with much light" (Hymn of the Greek Church to St. Thomas), and that light was the light of faith in Him Whom they had not seen. It is St. Thomas who comes today to revive our flagging faith, to introduce us to the Babe of Bethlehem and tell us that He is indeed the Orient though He is hiding His light, to warn us to give no heed to temptations against the faith, to tell us that when we are contemplating the humility and nothingness of our God and the temptation comes to us, as it did to him to say: Unless I see for myself, "I will not believe," to remember the words of the Master: "Blessed are they that have not seen and yet have believed."

O blessed Saint Thomas! who art now in the land of light and vision, intercede for us that we may be as little children, believing all we are told and quietly waiting till the day dawn and the Orient arises in all His majesty and strength, *preparing* as a giant to run His course, but for the moment hiding everything under the form of a helpless babe. We do not ask for sight but for the light which will lead us to Him, the light of faith, so that when we see Him wrapped in swaddling clothes and lying in a manger we may cry out with you: "My Lord and My God."

POINT III.
THE WAY OF PEACE.

The Orient visited us not only "to enlighten them that sit in darkness and in the shadow of death," but also "to direct our feet into the way of peace" (Luke 1: 79). And what is the way of peace but the way of *faith*, which He is coming to light up? Nothing can bring peace to this dark and sin-stricken world but faith. The Sun of Justice is rising with health in His Wings and that health is faith. It is the remedy for all ills. Men try every other remedy but they leave out God and His faith and the result is that the world remains in chaos. The Light has risen, the Orient has visited us, but men shut their eyes to the light and prefer the darkness, because their deeds are evil.

The *Way of Peace* is made by the Prince of Peace, it is the Highway to the Heaven of Peace. Am I on it? Yes, for I am one of "the household of faith" and can never thank Him sufficiently for having directed my feet into the City of Peace. But this is not all. Many people, even those of the "household of faith" have very little real peace in their lives. They spend their time in complaints, regrets, criticisms, anxieties. Is this what the King of Peace intends? Oh no! He is ever there waiting to direct their feet towards the "green pastures" and "the still waters," but the Way of Peace is the way of faith, of trust and confidence. Until I can really trust Him, the peaceful pastures can never be mine, I can never lie down in them and rest. I am His sheep, but I do not wholly trust my Shepherd. If I did, I should believe that whatever He chose and arranged for me was the best; I could not *complain* of what He had planned for me, however hard it might be. I could not criticize His arrangements and want to make my own. May my trust be so absolute this Christmas that it is apparent to everyone that I possess the peace which the Babe of Bethlehem comes to bring. O Orient come once more and direct my feet into the way of peace.

Colloquy with the Orient.

Resolution. "Although He should kill me, I will trust in Him." (Job. 13: 15).

Spiritual Bouquet. O Oriens!

— ❦ —

O Rex Gentium!

December 22nd.

"*O King of nations and their desired One and the Corner-stone that makest both one, come and save man whom Thou didst form out of slime!*" (Gen. 49: 10, Agg. 2: 8, Isaias 28: 16, Gen. 2: 7).

1st. *Prelude.* Mary and Joseph on the road to Bethlehem. "Behold thy King will come to thee.... He is poor and riding upon an ass." (Zach. 9: 9).

2nd. *Prelude.* Grace to welcome my King.

POINT I.
"THE DESIRED OF ALL NATIONS SHALL COME."

King of nations He has always been, for He created them; in Him they live and move and are. (Acts 17: 2). He has been in His earth ever since He created it, governing it, sustaining and preserving the life which He gave, co-operating always with His creatures. We must not think of Him as creating the world and then leaving it to do the best it could till the time came for Him to be incarnate. That is a false idea. His delights were *always* to be with the children of men and though the Orient did not begin to dawn till the time of the Incarnation, the Light had been in the world all along; the Sun of Justice had existed from all eternity. "He was in the world and the world was made by Him and the world knew Him not." (John 1: 10). But though it knew Him not, the world had enough light to desire Him. Ever since God at the time of man's fall had made His great promise concerning the Woman and her Seed, He that was to come had been to the nations "their desired One." That promise had been carefully cherished, handed on from father to son till Moses came and recorded it in the book of Genesis; and though of necessity one nation had to be selected to which the Woman and her Seed were to belong, yet the promise was given to all nations and all claimed their share in it. The chosen *nation* through whom all the others were to be blessed was Abraham's. Through him and his seed the great promise was to be fulfilled (Gen. 12: 3). The *time* was hinted at in the patriarch Jacob's blessing to Juda: "The sceptre shall not be taken away from Juda, nor a ruler from his thigh, till He come that is to be sent and He shall be the expectation of nations" (Gen. 49: 10). The house or *family* which was to have the joy of realizing the promise was David's; the *place* where the Woman was to bring forth her Seed was Bethlehem. Here "she that travaileth shall bring forth" and here "shall He come ... that is to be the Ruler in Israel" (Mich. 5: 2-3). Each subsequent prophecy or promise developed and enlarged the original one given in Eden, but in that one the nations had all that they needed upon which to build up their hopes and nourish their desires—the Woman and her Seed, the "Child with His Mother"—and though the promise *belonged* to the chosen nation (Rom. 9: 4), the first great promise had been handed down through the other nations and they knew enough to make them *desire*, enough to find the Light if they sought it as did the Wise Kings of the East.

O King of nations, as I look back through the ages and see the Child and His Mother so clearly set forth in promise and prophecy, in type and example, when I think of Thy plans for the redemption of the world, made from all eternity and gradually unfolding as the fulness of time approached, when I think of the nations all desiring Thy coming, when I think of the intense desire of Thy loving Heart, there is one thing that seems to jar and to be out of harmony with the rest, and that is the lamentable want of desire in my own heart! The time is very short now, the Child with His Mother are already on the way to Bethlehem. Oh! Let me multiply my Acts of Desire that my little King when He comes may be indeed *my* "desired One" too. "I sat down under His shadow, Whom I desired." (Cant. 2: 3).

POINT II.

THE CORNER-STONE THAT MAKETH BOTH ONE.

"Behold I will lay a stone in the foundations of Sion, a tried stone, a corner-stone, a precious stone, founded in the foundations" (Isaias 28: 16), "the stone which the builders rejected" (Ps. 117: 22).

This is one of the promises confided to the chosen nation. Our Blessed Lord claims it as applying to Himself (Matt. 21: 42, Luke 20: 17), and St. Peter and St. Paul both speak of it as if it were well known. (Acts 4: 11, 1 Peter 2: 6-8, Rom. 9: 33, Eph. 2: 20).

He is the Corner-stone Who is coming to make both one (Eph. 2: 14), both the Jews to whom belongs the promise (Rom. 9: 4) and the Gentiles who are "co-partners of His promise" (Eph. 3: 6). He is coming to preach peace to them that are far off as well as to them that are nigh, coming to make "the strangers and foreigners" feel that they are "fellow-citizens with the saints and the domestics of God," coming to weld all together into one great building of which He Him-self is to be the chief Corner-stone, binding together the two walls (Jews and Gentiles), supporting each stone and keeping each in its place, a holy temple in the Lord, "a habitation of God in the spirit." Such is the picture St. Paul draws for us (Eph. 2), and such is the picture which the antiphon for today brings before our minds. "All one in Christ Jesus." He is the King of all nations, the Desired of all nations, the Corner-stone of the whole building; with Him there is neither Jew nor Gentile (Gal. 3: 28).

Let me tell Him even now before He comes how I long to share in the great work so dear to His Sacred Heart, let me offer myself to co-operate with Him in His designs for the human race which He loves so well.

Let me be ready to labour, to suffer, to pray, to spend and be spent, if only I may thus bring Him a few stones for His Holy Temple. I was "sometime afar off" but now have been "made nigh by the Blood of Christ" (Eph. 2: 13). "What shall I render?" (Ps. 115: 12).

Point III.

Come And Save Man Whom Thou Didst Form Out of The Dust.

"Their desired One" Who has never been far from the hearts of His children, knows the need of the nations. He Who formed man out of the dust knows his need of a Saviour. What are the desires of the nations compared with His desire? From all eternity He has desired the time to come when by taking the nature of man He could fulfil their desires and be to them both

135

a King and a Saviour. Very soon now will the Angels be telling the glad tidings to man: To you is born the Saviour. Very soon will the heavenly choirs be singing the praises of the new-born King, and the question will be asked even by distant nations: "Where is He that is born King?"

Oh! come, little King, come and fulfil the desires of all hearts. Thou hast given them and Thou also must satisfy them. Art Thou really the one desire of my heart, around which all my hopes centre? If Thou wert not there, I know that life would be nothing but a blank. Come and create a greater desire than ever after the perfection Thou wouldst have, and then show me how to follow after it. "In what place soever Thou shalt be, my Lord King ... there will Thy servant be" (2 Kings 15: 21). Today then I will journey with Thy blessed Mother, for surely the closer I keep to her, the greater must be my desires.

Colloquy with "the desired One."
Resolution. Grace to desire Him more ardently.
Spiritual Bouquet. O Rex Gentium!

— ❦ —

O Emmanuel!

December 23rd.

"O Emmanuel, our King and Lawgiver, the Expectation and Saviour of the nations! Come and save us, O Lord our God." (Is. 7: 14, 8: 8, 33: 22, Jas. 4: 12).

> *1st. Prelude.* Mary and Joseph in the temple at Jerusalem.
> *2nd. Prelude.* Grace to worship with them.

POINT I.
EMMANUEL, GOD WITH US.

On the way from Nazareth to Bethlehem lies Jerusalem and we may be quite sure that a happy event for Mary and Joseph on this long and tiring journey now nearing its end would be their visit to the Temple, near which Mary, and probably Joseph too, had spent most of her life. We may think, then, of Mary today taking her Son into His own Temple. We may think of the joy of the Angels as they lifted high the gates to let the hidden King come in. In the Holy of Holies of Solomon's Temple was the Ark of the Covenant, inside which were the Tables of God's law and upon which was manifested the presence of the All-Holy. But here kneeling in the Temple, in the women's court afar off, was the real Ark of the Covenant of which the other was only a type, hiding within her chaste womb the new Lawgiver Whose Presence was known only to the Angels who were worshipping round His Shrine, and to Mary and Joseph the only earthly worshippers in the Temple that day who understood.

Here was the Virgin with her Son, the prophecy was fulfilled—God with us. "His name shall be called *Emmanuel.*"

Yet Mary and Joseph were not the only worshippers in the Temple that day—there was a Human Soul worshipping God as He had never been worshipped before. The Heart of Jesus now so near the end of the first stage of Its existence on earth was offering to God all Its homage and all Its love, offering to Him all the work that had been done during the nine months passed in the holy "Ark of the Covenant," all the humiliation and self-abasement, the silence and dependence, the suffering and patience, the satisfaction and merit. He had been doing all the time the things that pleased His Father, the things that He had made Himself man to be able to do.

Now He is waiting—and the very waiting is another Act of worship—waiting for the moment to come when He can take the next step in His earthly journey, waiting with His Mother whose intense desire is only second to His Own.

O Emmanuel! God with us! I feel that I must go too to Thy Sacred Courts today and make one more worshipper before that Holy Shrine. Advent is nearly over, my time of preparation is well-nigh at an end. What have I to offer as I kneel in adoration? Feeble desires, broken resolutions, failure again in the thing I did so want not to fail in this Advent, good intentions, but little else. Dare I come and kneel there where all is so holy and so perfect? Yes, for He is *Emmanuel*, God incarnate for me. Let me hand Him through His Mother all my poverty and wretchedness and weakness and failure, together with my contrition and repentance and love, and in exchange He will hand me His forgiveness and the promise to offer my inadequate worship, together with His own Divine perfections, to His Father, Who will be satisfied. This is what *Emmanuel* means.

POINT II.
OUR LAWGIVER.

"The Lord is our Judge, the Lord is our Lawgiver, the Lord is our King He will save us." (Is. 33: 22).

He is our King, therefore He has a right to make laws for us. And who could be a better Judge of how the laws are kept than He Who made them? Am I afraid at the sterner aspect which things seem to have taken? There is no need, for He is still our *Emmanuel*, but He can only be thus our Friend and Companion by being also the One Who has an absolute right to make laws for us and to expect our obedience. "You are My *friends*, if you do the things I command you" (John 15: 14).

The reason for *all* His titles is that He wills to *save* us. He is first of all the Saviour and then, in order that our salvation may be accomplished, He makes Himself our King, our Lawgiver and finally our Judge. "If you love Me, keep My commandments." Such is our Lawgiver's appeal. Surely His commandments are not grievous. He Who did always the things which pleased His Father, asks us to try to do the same.

O my little Lawgiver, accomplishing so silently and so perfectly the Will of Thy Father, command me and I will obey, give Thy orders through whom Thou wilt; be they hard or easy, be they in accordance with my will or contrary to my whole nature! I will think of Thy perfect submission to Thy Father's Will during those nine months for me and will say: I, too, will do always the things which please Him no matter what they cost.

POINT III.

THE EXPECTATION OF THE NATIONS.

JESUS is waiting, Mary is waiting, the Angels are waiting, all nations, all the earth, and Heaven too is waiting—waiting for our Emmanuel to come and save us. The empty manger speaks of the Church's expectation today. We can count the hours now, all things are ready. Oh! come and save us! Come and begin Thy blessed work over again, come and save the many who as yet know Thee not and who are expecting everything this Christmas *except* a Saviour. May the sight of the empty crib remind me to look well into my preparations today to see that nothing is wanting in the welcome I am going to give to the King!

> *Colloquy* with our Emmanuel. At the Incarnation, at Thy birth, all through Thy life, Thou didst dwell *with us*; on every altar Thou hast promised to be

with us all days; in Holy Communion Thou hast
said I will dwell *with them*; in the hour of death
I will fear no evil for Thou wilt be *with me*; and
Thou hast secured Heaven for me by Thy prayer:
"Father, I will that those whom Thou hast given
Me be *with Me* where I am." "Emmanuel, *God
with us*."

Resolution. Grace to expect Him today in all that I do.
Spiritual Bouquet. O Emmanuel!

— ❧ —

Christmas Eve.

December 24th.

*"This day you shall know that the Lord will come and save us:
and in the morning you shall see His glory."* (Ex. 16. "Introit" for
Christmas Eve).

1st. Prelude. The stable and the manger waiting for JESUS.
2nd. Prelude. Grace to make my final preparations.

POINT I.
MY PREPARATION—LAST TOUCHES.

Today Mary and Joseph arrive at their journey's end. We
think of them footsore, weary, homeless; we think of the discouragement and rebuffs that they meet with as they hear
on all sides that there is no room for them; but do we think
enough of the intense joy that reigned in Mary's heart, a
joy communicated to her by her Son? He is rejoicing that
His hour is come; the very refusals of His people to receive
Him and His Mother are to Him a sign that His work has
begun and is already being opposed. Mary shares His joy;

she is absorbed by one thought—soon she will look upon His Face—and that thought is so great that there is scarcely room for any other in her heart. And Joseph? Can we imagine him anxious and disturbed and worried? No, it is impossible—he is with JESUS and Mary, he has lived his life close to them for nine months, he has imbibed their spirit. If his joy is not as intense as theirs, his *peace* is unruffled; he has brought the Mother with her Child to Bethlehem as he was told to do, and he knows that God will take care of His own.

My first lessons, then, for today are apparent. In the morning I shall see His glory; the Point of Advent is reached, my preparation is nearly over. I was told to get ready for Him, I was told to come to Bethlehem, I have been trying to do so, trying to keep up with Mary and Joseph on their journey; often, I am obliged to admit it, it has been a following afar off, but still by God's grace, I *am* following and I know that today He is coming to save us and that tomorrow I shall see His glory for He will come to me in Holy Communion. He will be born again in my heart and make me understand once more that He is incarnate for me. Are my joy and my peace so great that nothing has the power to touch them? There are many occupations that must of necessity claim my time and my attention today, as there were many coming and going on the roads that led to Bethlehem; there are many things to be thought about in my last preparations for Christmas—it was so with Mary and Joseph too. Almost certainly I shall have today, as they had, things that try and weary me, perhaps suffering, temptation, slights and even insults. Shall I receive them as last and most precious opportunities for adding the finishing touches to my preparation, for gaining a victory where I have perhaps so recently lost one, for making reparation to my King and for uniting myself more closely to Him and His Mother? Will the thought that He is coming be so absorbing that the difficulties of the way are hardly noticed or are welcome as a reminder that I too am journeying to Bethlehem? If I cannot aspire to the joy of JESUS and Mary, I can at least aim at the peace of St. Joseph.

POINT II.

HIS PREPARATION.

His preparation is coming to an end too. Let me go over in my mind once again all that He had to plan and to do by way of preparation before He could come to me in Holy Communion. It was for this that the Incarnation was a preparation. In order to feed me with His Flesh and Blood, He had to become incarnate. This is the Point of Christmas, and it is the Point of contact between JESUS and my soul. Tomorrow Mary in an ecstasy of joy will look upon His Face and press Him to her heart; tomorrow Joseph, full of awe and wonder, will take Him in his arms; tomorrow the Angels will sing their *Glorias* as they gaze upon their God incarnate; tomorrow the shepherds will adore and offer Him their gifts; and tomorrow I too shall touch Him very closely for I shall receive into my body and into my heart His Body and Blood, His Soul and His Divinity. He will be with me and I with Him. It is for this that I have been making my preparations and it is for this that He has been making His. How long has He been preparing? Not only during Advent, not only during the nine months, not only since the great promise was given in Eden, not only since the time when there was war among the Angels because of the Incarnation—I am getting beyond time already and farther back than that I cannot go for my mind is finite; but His is infinite and just because it is infinite there never was a time when the Incarnation was not in His mind, and there never was a time when I, His child, was not

142

in His mind, and also there never was a time when He did not see the blest moments when He should bring the two into contact and make me understand personally what the Point of the Incarnation is. These blest moments are my Communions and surely one of the most blest must be my Christmas Communion when He Who comes to me and Who feeds me with Himself is the Child Who was born at Bethlehem, He Who had been so long expected, the Seed of the Woman, the Orient from on high, the Star of the East, the Desired One of the nations, the Root of Jesse, the King of the Gentiles with His Key and His Sceptre, Emmanuel, God with us.

Colloquy. I kneel at the door of the empty stable and offer Thee my heart, O my little JESUS! I have tried to make room for Thee; I have made my poor little preparations with Thy blessed Mother; I have taken long journeys to get to Thee; but my body is not fit to be Thy temple and my heart is treacherous and faithless. I am ashamed to have so poor a shelter to offer Thee. If it were not that Thou didst ask for it, I dare not offer it. Oh! Thou Who didst not refuse the manger-bed, come to my heart, look at the contrition and the humiliation and the reparation and the aching longing to be what Thou dost want, and forget the faithlessness and the failures and the weakness. Come, my little King, incarnate for me, come and save me, if I were not a sinner I should not need a Saviour.

Resolution. To keep very near to Mary and Joseph today.
Spiritual Bouquet. "In the morning you shall see His glory."

Courtesy of *Campion Missal and Hymnal*

www.ingramcontent.com/pod-product-compliance
Lightning Source LLC
La Vergne TN
LVHW021459080426
835509LV00018B/2346